Hans, __ was great
meeting you up AT Malibu,
may God Bless your
re-election effort

Letters
to
My Son,

Keep Being A light
in Dark places,

Jamie

Hard Earned Lessons from a Slow Learner

Letters
to
My Son

Jamie Bohnett

WinePressPublishing
Great Books, Defined.

WinePress Publishing (PO Box 428, Enumclaw, WA 98022) functions only as a book publisher. As such, the ultimate design, content, editorial accuracy, and views expressed or implied in this work are those of the author.

Unless otherwise noted, all Scriptures are taken from the *Holy Bible, New International Version®, NIV®*. Copyright © 1973, 1978, 1984 by Biblica, Inc.™ Used by permission of Zondervan. All rights reserved worldwide. www.zondervan.com

Scripture references marked KJV are taken from the *King James Version* of the Bible.

Scripture references marked NASB are taken from the *New American Standard Bible*, © 1960, 1963, 1968, 1971, 1972, 1973, 1975, 1977 by The Lockman Foundation. Used by permission.

ISBN 13: 978-1-4141-2030-0
ISBN 10: 1-4141-2030-3
Library of Congress Catalog Card Number: 2011920761

Contents

"This little book is dedicated to my two sons, Adam and Jeremy. I am so thankful for you both and for what you have taught me as boys and now as young men."

—Dad

Introduction

*M*Y WIFE, CINDY, and I have two sons, Adam and Jeremy. Adam has graduated from Whitworth University and is making his way working at a restaurant and developing his interests in music and photography. Jeremy is pursuing a business degree as he plays baseball at Harding University in Arkansas. These two young men, along with our daughter, Heidi, our son-in-law, Sky, our granddaughters, Ellie and Sadie, and our youngest daughter, Holly, who also attends Harding University, are the great joys of our lives. (And as of this writing, we eagerly await the arrival of our third grandchild...a grandson!)

My sons are beginning to navigate the challenges of young adulthood, and there are many choices and opportunities before them. What will they wind up doing for their career? Who will they marry? Will they have children? And if they do, How many? Where will they eventually live? These and many more decisions are theirs. In fact, the decisions they both make in the next five to ten years will greatly influence the following fifty years. And because I have a biblical worldview, I believe their choices will effect eternity.

What I desire to communicate to them—and to every young adult male who reads this book—is not so much what I desire for them to *do*, but rather who I desire them to *be*. I don't know what God has for them or the readers to *do* in their lives, because that is an unfolding mystery that each of us needs to discover. However, I am confident that I know what they are all to *be*. I know this because some things are universal. I believe the doing (vocation, marriage, children, etc.) will naturally, or should I say supernaturally, unfold out of their being this type of men.

The ideas for this book came out of a five-year period when I wrote about the challenges of family life in a blog I called "Father Power." I discovered upon reflection that these blogs contain clear themes that reveal, I believe, not just "a father's heart" but "the heavenly Father's heart" for each of His sons. As my two sons began launching their lives, I wanted to re-write these blogs into direct messages to them, so they would know my heart of love for them, my faith in their God's sufficiency, and hope for their futures. Since I have sought to base these upon the Scriptures and to listen to God's Spirit as I wrote them, I believe these writings more importantly reflect their heavenly Father's heart for each of my boys.

If Adam and Jeremy are the only ones to read this book and take my words to heart, I will have accomplished my goal. But I believe that my sons represent many other young adult men who are trying to find their way through a maze of confusion that discourages and clouds a clear vision of the development of lasting godly character.

I address the messages in the singular form as in "Dear Son," which applies to both of my sons, rather than going back and forth to Adam and Jeremy. This is a technique that King Solomon employed in the book of Proverbs by repeatedly saying "My Son" or "Dear Son" (singular). He may have had one "son" in mind when he penned his words but he has had many "sons" throughout history who have gained wisdom from his words. I think this is a worthy model to follow.

I have divided the thirty-nine letters in this book into twelve chapters. It is my prayer for all who would read my letters that you would hear the Father's heart in them, and that through His Son, Jesus, each of you would become His dear son as well. You are loved and His beloved! You are accepted in His Son. You can live out your life *from* acceptance, not *for* acceptance. In the heavenly Father's heart, you are truly His "Dear Son."

For those of you who do not have a close relationship with your father, it is my prayer that you will allow me to speak to you as a kind of "stand-in father." And for those of you who do have a good relationship with your father, I pray that these letters will reinforce the things he has sought to teach you.

In my letters I reveal my own struggles as a father, so perhaps you will be able to see a little reflection of your own father's life, and gain some insight and perspective into the challenges that he faced. Throughout the book I hope you will see my love for my sons, and you will come to know that my love is just a fraction of the love our heavenly Father has for each of His sons, which includes you! St. Augustine proclaimed that, "God loves every one of us as if there were but one of us to love." I have grown to believe this and I hope you will too.

We live in a world that heaps so much pressure upon each of us to "measure up." I pray that the things I talk about in this book will provide you peace knowing that in the Father's eyes, because of what His beloved Son has done for you, you *already* do measure up.

I am asking the Father to secure you in His love as you reflect on the messages in these letters. And I'm trusting that my messages will be like "wind words" for the sail of your soul as you move out of the safe harbor of the home into the challenging journey of adulthood.

—**Jamie Bohnett**
June 2011

Chapter 1

God Made You
One of a Kind

"Don't ask yourself what the world needs; ask yourself what makes you come alive. And then go and do that—because the world needs people who have come alive."
—Harold Whitman

Hearing the Same Words Differently

Dear Son,

A few years ago when you were younger, I was going through a period of depression. I decided to see a counselor. This brash young man said to me, "You don't know who you are." I didn't see him as a man who really cared about me or believed in me, so his words stung me as an indictment. I interpreted them to mean, "You are not authentic and real. You are a pretender." It felt like I had just been kicked in the stomach. Now, not only was I a depressed person, but I was someone who didn't have a clue who he was and was about sixty-five bucks poorer!

As I chewed on that counselor's message a few days later (after I got over my anger!) I was able to hear his words again with different ears. This time I heard the gentle voice of the heavenly Father speaking the same words but with a completely different meaning! I heard, "You don't know who you are; if you did you wouldn't need to wallow in depression and self-doubt. You would rejoice in the incredible, high and exalted, beloved place you have of simply being My son! The enemy wants to obscure your amazing identity from your soul. Don't let him, son! Trust what I have said about you in My word. Choose to believe it. *This* is reality. Please let it sink in, My beloved son."

The same words now held a totally different message. What made the difference? One message was spoken by someone whom I perceived as a distant and critical professional. The other was spoken by a committed, believing-the-best-in-me Father. One messenger seemed to see me burdened with a history, but the Father spoke to me as one blessed with a destiny.

As you are launching into your adult life, I tell you honestly that *you* really don't know who you are yet. Please don't hear my words as a criticism. You aren't a phony. However, you are just beginning to discover the wonder of all God has created and redeemed you uniquely to be. He sees you as a man of destiny. Son, all of your past has prepared you and is now pointing you to fulfill an amazing future—in this life and in the life to come. I say that with confidence because I know that you belong to a God who is "able to do immeasurably more than all we ask or imagine, according to his power that is at work within us" (Ephesians 3:20).

Benjamin Disraeli said, "The greatest good you can do for another is not just to share your riches, but to reveal to him his own." That is what I am seeking to do through these letters, son; I want to help you begin to see how "rich" you really are.

Believing in you,

Dad

School Daze and the Comparison Trap

Dear Son,

Do you remember your K-12 school days? Good luck with trying to forget them. Like so many others, I've been trying to process my school days (school daze) ever since I have been out of school, and I think a lot of the pain I went through has to do with "the comparison trap." School is all about comparison from the get go. Comparison takes place in four broad categories: academic performance, athletic ability, physical attractiveness, and social standing. The problem with this as I see it, son, is it sets us up for the compulsion to compare throughout our adulthood. This isn't just a childhood issue!

I have experienced both sides of this trap. I believe the problem originates from a sense of identity that is rooted in what other people think of me, whether positive or negative. This is the "fear of man" that Solomon warned us about in his book of Proverbs, "Fear of man will prove to be a snare, but whoever trusts in the LORD is kept safe" (Proverbs 29:25).

Let me explain to you how this works. First, we often think *less* of ourselves when we compare ourselves academically, athletically, physically, or socially with another. When we do this we allow another person's strengths to rob us of the joy of being who God has created us to be. We begin to secretly root for their failure when we should instead be celebrating their successes with them—as well as our own.

3

We don't see our own growth and improvement because we compare it to someone who is more successful, gifted, or blessed in a certain area.

The other side of this danger is that we allow strength in a certain area to create pride and a sense of superiority over others, to think *more* of ourselves and less about our need to depend upon God. Both are equally dangerous, but the latter is not mentioned as much in our self-esteem obsessed culture.

Here is the thing, son, that I want to warn you about from my own experience: Once we begin to believe that we need to be "successful" in all we do so that we feel good about ourselves, then we become addicted to the approval of others. It is hard to be real and transparent, because we want to keep up the "appearance" of success. Consequently, we find it hard to reveal our true selves to others. We become like Moses who veiled his fading glory after coming down the mountaintop, working hard to keep up his false front while slowly dying inside. We also tend to accept others on the basis of their performance or appearance, not their innate worth.

I confess that I have struggled with the comparison trap throughout my life. I know that much of it was rooted in believing the childhood lie that I was not a unique, one-of-a-kind-son of the Father, who is unconditionally loved by Him through success or failure. This made me concern myself too much with how others reacted to me, affirmed me, or appreciated me.

For me, son, I have found the best thing that I can do to overcome in this area is to redirect my focus to what God has said about me in His word, and allow those truths to slowly soak into the depths of my soul. Here are a couple of Bible passages that I have found helpful:

Make a careful exploration of who you are and the work
you have been given, and then sink yourself into that.
Don't be impressed with yourself. Don't compare yourself
with others. Each of you must take responsibility for
doing the creative best you can with your own life.
                                    —Galatians 6:4-5, The Message

Let's just go ahead and be what we were made to be,
without enviously or pridefully comparing ourselves with
each other, or trying to be something we aren't.
                                    —Romans 12:6, The Message

Work out your own salvation, son, because it is God who
is within you both to will (want) and do (accomplish)
His good pleasure!
                                    —Philippians 2:12-13, your dad's version!

                         Celebrating *you*,

                         Dad

Ordinary Guys, Frogs, and Lizards

Dear Son,

You have grown up in a world that worships celebrity. A
few people seem to be lifted up, whether in sports, politics,
business, or religion, while the rest of the teeming anonymous
masses bow down in worship to them. This really bothers me
because, as I have already written, every one of us is uniquely
created in God's image to worship Him alone.

The one area where this really irks me is when I see this
tendency in the evangelical Christian sub-culture. This is
the one place that "idol worship" should not take place!
If God has any favorites (and He doesn't), He really seems
to show an amazing preference for the ordinary, the small,
the weak, the wounded, the neglected, the ignored, the

disrespected, the damaged, the down and counted out. The Bible emphatically states this, and when we see who tend to be drawn to Him we can observe this to be true.

As Abraham Lincoln said about common people, we can say about we who are ordinary Christians: "He must love us as He has made so many of us!" This is Jesus' way. This is His way of spreading His presence and glory through every nook and cranny of the world and taking ordinary people to fill workplaces, schools, recreational teams, neighborhoods, etc. with *Him*. His extraordinariness shines best through the ordinary.

I heard a story that I'd like to relate to you, son, as I think it paints a good picture of how God works through the ordinary guy. The story came through a speaker at a worldwide missions conference. He compared the frog and the lizard. The frog's way of eating is to stay in one place and wait for unsuspecting "food" to come to him. If he tried to hop all around the pond or along the shore he would starve. He is just too bulky a presence. The lizard is different. He can squeeze into any place imaginable; into palaces, shacks, fields, or rocks, to get his meals.

The frog is the most visible, but the lizard covers the most ground. Our Christian sub-culture glorifies "frogs," those who are in the limelight, gifted crowd-gatherers, and downplays the "lizards." The "frogs" do have an important place in God's kingdom, but it is the lizard that can go where no frog could ever go. To me, the lizard is like the "ordinary guy."

You see, son, God uses ordinary guys like you and me to show an unbelieving world that is often tired of *hearing* the message of Christ's salvation, but is open to *seeing* the difference He makes in our lives as we handle stress, conflict, temptation, success, failure, disappointment, sickness, death, and everything in between. Ordinary guys allow God to be seen up close and personal. Through ordinary guys, through "lizards," the light of Christ is carried into the darkest of places, where His light is needed the most.

> "Jesus lived the ordinary life of men of his time, in order to sanctify the ordinary lives of men of all times."
> —Thomas Merton

An ordinary guy with an extraordinary God,
Dad

We Become What We Think We Are

Dear Son,

As a father I have had the privilege (yes, I say "privilege") of walking with one of my children through the journey of addiction recovery. It is not a journey that we chose to walk, but walk it we did. The first few weeks of learning of this addiction was a nightmare for us all. I remember being in a daze when we went to that first parent information meeting for the outpatient program. A smiling, vibrant woman met your mother and me in the hallway and escorted us into a room with some others. She offered us pizza and pop, and we sat down with the others in the room.

I looked around and thought, *This is weird. Are these parents of kids with drug and alcohol issues?* They seemed pretty happy and upbeat. One person asked me what kind of work I did. It seemed odd for that to be the first question to be asked in a group like this. After eating some pizza, I finally realized that we had actually walked into a "net users group." I had heard the lady say "users" and "group" and I assumed this was the parents group for kids in recovery from drugs and alcohol.

Taking the pizza and pop in hand, we laughed and told them that we were in the wrong group as we meekly walked out of the room…backwards! I told Cindy that someday we would laugh at that mix up that gave us some free pizza. We never did find the right group that night and I'm still waiting for her to be able to laugh about the episode.

Later on I did attend the parent's week, where I educated myself about the problem of addiction. This was not a faith-based program, so they were coming from a different worldview than I have, but they did have some good wisdom and information. But one thing I couldn't swallow was a comment from one of the instructors. She was telling a story and she referred to our kids as "your little addicts."

I refuse to believe that my child would be always defined as a "little addict." I have since learned that through God's grace a person who struggles with addiction can come to the place of referring to himself or herself as a recovered or recovering addict. Now that doesn't mean that the person doesn't need to walk through the God-dependent steps and stay sober, while recognizing the pull towards addiction will always be there. But it does mean that he or she does not need to be defined by their addiction.

Does that make sense, son? We become who we think we are.

I have a friend who has a ministry to men who struggle with same-sex attraction. He doesn't refer to himself or those he helps as "gay" or "homosexual" because these are identity words. Once a person allows himself to be labeled with an identity, then behavior will naturally flow out of it. In other words, it is legitimate to admit to struggling in a certain area, but it is harmful to allow that struggle to define who you are as a person.

The following passage of Scripture has been helpful to me in this regard:

Do you not know that the wicked will not inherit the kingdom of God? Do not be deceived: Neither the sexually immoral nor idolaters nor adulterers nor male prostitutes nor homosexual offenders nor thieves nor the greedy nor drunkards nor slanderers nor swindlers will inherit the kingdom of God. *And that is what some of you were.* But you were washed, you were sanctified, you were justified in the name of the Lord Jesus Christ and by the Spirit of our God.

—1 Corinthians 6:9-11, emphasis added

The apostle Paul acknowledged that the Corinthians had indulged in some pretty nasty sins, but that behavior no longer defined them. This identity was past tense. Because of their trust in the sacrifice of God's Son and the renewal of the Holy Spirit in their lives, their identity was changed forever.

Our identity, how we see ourselves, is a powerful thing for evil but also for good. Once we grasp our true identity, our behavior will flow from out of who we see that we are. The Father living in me could not and would not accept that my child was "a little addict." Past behavior, no matter how addictive, habitual, or destructive will *never* define the heavenly Father's kids!

My life is no longer defined by what I have done, good or bad, or what has been done to me, good or bad, but by what Christ has done for me and what He does through me. I have found this to be a freeing way to live. I know that you will too!

Believing in who God says you are,

Dad

Chapter 2

Weakness: The Key to True Manly Strength

"Build me a son, O Lord, who will be strong enough to know when he is weak, and brave enough to face himself when he is afraid; one who will be proud and unbending in honest defeat, and humble and gentle in victory."
—Gen. Douglas MacArthur

Father Power or Father Weakness?

Dear Son,

Your mother and I used to think of being a parent much differently than we do today. We thought about it much more like following a formula. If we did "A" plus "B" the result would be "C." For those who didn't get the desired results, they were either not fully buying into the formula or they believed the formula but were not properly applying it; they were using some "wrong formula" or they were just winging it!

Now that all of our children are into adulthood, we have finally realized what we should have realized years ago:

The whole formula thing doesn't work the way it has been heralded to work. I know that throwing out formulas can be seen by some as just giving up on "principled parenting," but I'm sorry, children aren't appliances; they come with no guarantees. Being a father of adult children is a much more "out of control" experience than I believed it to be when I was younger.

When I was in the midst of a time of uncertainty in our family journey, a good friend emailed me. "Be strong for your wife and weak for God," he said. That was helpful to hear and reminded me that my strength needs to be from God and not some kind of false bravado. Since that time, I have clung to 2 Corinthians 12:9a: "But he said to me, 'My grace is sufficient for you, for my power is made perfect in weakness.'"

I heard a Christian recently say that we need to learn to sit with God and "only have questions." Sometimes on this life journey questions are all we have. For example, when Job was going through his stuff he never learned the "why" or the "how long" regarding his suffering. Doesn't it seem more than a little inconsiderate from our perspective that God wouldn't fill him in with what was going on behind the scenes, and how He planned for everything to come out as it did? Apparently, our heavenly Father finds answering the "whys" and the "how longs" counterproductive when He is teaching His children important lessons on trust.

Son, now that I'm a dad, I'm reminded of the heartache I caused my mother as a rebellious teen. I was pretty immune to my mother's pleading and cajoling but I *could not* resist her prayers. I can remember feeling some kind of invisible rope just as I was hitting a limit of my rebellion that pulled me back to a desperate dependence upon God. This happened even as I seemed to try my best to move away from Him. Little did I know that my mother and her friends formed a commando-like band of Christian women who prayed down the strongholds that held me captive to the enemy's ways. For years I have prayed for you and your siblings in the same way. Lucky you, eh?!

Son, I needed to learn what all of us as men must learn if we want to know God as our Father and Best Friend. As F. B. Meyer said, we "must get to the end of ourselves before He (Christ) can begin in us." Oswald Chambers said it like this: "The greatest blessing spiritually is the knowledge that we are destitute; until we get there, our Lord is powerless."

Just as I needed to learn this in my youth, I need to learn this again as your dad. I am powerless to teach you the lessons of powerlessness! It is a very painful thing for me to ask for God to do this in your life, because I know from personal experience what it can mean. But I can pray no greater blessings upon you, son. I write this to you to encourage you and remind you that the very things that may be confounding you, confusing you, and frustrating you are the vehicles your loving Father has allowed into your life to teach you your utter need for *Him*. This need is not just for your eternal salvation, but also for your daily bread.

My father power will best help you when you understand my father weakness, because there I find true strength that comes from His Son.

Entrusting you into His all-capable hands,

Dad

Tailor-Made Repentance

Dear Son,

Did you ever think that your path to growth into Christ-likeness is "tailor-made" just for you? You have inherited sinful tendencies from me as well as some good qualities that reflect the heavenly Father. You can thank the Lord for whatever good that you have gleaned from my life. But be aware; I am a sinful man and have passed on some tendencies that I never intended to.

It is your job to sort through all that and to assess the good and the bad, so that you can build upon the good that I have taught you. Take it a step further on your journey and allow those qualities to be even greater than I have cultivated in my own life. But turn away from the bad. I learned tendencies from my father and he learned them from his father. Each generation impacts the next. Ask God to reveal to you what you need to turn away from in repentance that you have most likely "caught" from me. Please forgive me for what I unintentionally passed on to you. You will need to turn from that attitude, habit, or tendency and ask your heavenly Father to graciously redirect you, through His gracious Spirit of Sonship that lives in you.

This all doesn't seem fair does it? But this is how we are to walk down that centerline with the tension of honoring our parents on one side and "hating" them on the other. I believe that "hating" them is a metaphor for putting Christian discipleship above allegiance to them and the attitudes and actions that they inadvertently passed on to us.

Reflect on what I am saying, son. This is important. This will guide you to focus on the most important areas that God wants to both build into you (where you are strong already) and those He wants to tear down so He can replace new, Christ-like qualities in you.

Trusting you will take this to heart,

Dad

The Protruding Plank

Dear Son,

I just wrote on Facebook® that, "There are two things that I hate to experience when I am driving: "#1—People who tailgate me and #2—When I tailgate people and they slow down." I'm sure you get the point. It is easy to be critical of others and be completely blind to our own wrong attitude or behavior. I wonder why it is so easy to blame others (whom I can't control) while denying my own responsibility (which I can control).

Sometimes I get upset at how kids today fail to take personal responsibility. But I need to take a look at the log in my own eye. What have I modeled? When I am wrong, do I always humbly ask for forgiveness? I believe I usually do eventually, but it isn't my first natural response, that's for sure. I believe this is part of our fallen condition, son.

For years I have spoken to men and this is one area where we as men have some poor role models from our fathers. Very few men have fathers who showed them how to humble themselves and ask for forgiveness when they were wrong. It is a generational curse of stubborn pride.

14

Son, please forgive me for all of the times when I have been your "speck inspector," while ignoring the protruding plank sticking out of my own eye! I know I have done this and I am so sorry.

In humble need of your forgiveness,

Dad

Chapter 3

Becoming the Right Guy Is Even More Important than Finding the Right Girl

"By all means marry; if you get a good wife, you'll become happy; if you get a bad one, you'll become a philosopher."
—Socrates

Marriage Motivation for a Lifetime

Dear Son,

Your mom and I were deeply moved when we watched the film, "The Notebook" on our 30th wedding anniversary. What really touched me was how the man, Noah, played by James Garner, sacrificially loved his wife through the disease of dementia to the very end. There clearly was very little in the relationship left for him, except the pain of being a stranger to the one woman he had loved his entire adult life.

Son, the problem with most marriage books on the market is their primary appeal to self-fulfillment. They make the false assumption that a lifetime marriage is the primary path to one's happiness. The emphases in these books are on things like conflict resolution, healthy communication, sexual techniques, and understanding male-female differences. While these things are all very important, they cannot touch a man's deepest motivation to love his wife for a lifetime. They cannot make a man into a "Noah."

I have grown to see that marriage is God's gift to me to learn practically how to love another person sacrificially, while growing to understand the heavenly Father's love for me through His Son. The challenge of learning to love one woman for a lifetime, until death separates us, causes what I have known intellectually about God's sacrificial love for me to be absorbed into the very depths of my mind and heart. Also, as I grow in my insight into Christ's love for us as a couple, I'm empowered to love your mother freely from the heart as the two work together.

Son, since you were born, I have been praying for you, for God to bring a godly woman into your life to be your wife. I don't minimize the importance of that choice. Next to the choice to follow Jesus Christ as your Lord, this choice is your life's most important. I have been forever blessed by marrying your mom at the tender (and naïve) age of nineteen. You and your siblings are a combination of our genes. I really can't imagine what my life would have been like without her. Can you imagine your life without her as your mom?

But as important as that choice is, let me say that your commitment to become the man that God desires you to be within your marriage, no matter how difficult, is even more important than choosing the "perfect partner." How can I say that? Because, no matter how wonderful your wife may be, you will discover that she has many weaknesses and areas that will rub you the wrong way. That is just how marriage is. God designed it that way so we will learn His kind of love: that agape love that sacrifices for the other. As soon as you can come to peace with this—and forget about the myth of "finding the perfect woman"—the better!

> Always seeking to become a better husband,
> Dad

Every Marriage Needs Renewal

Dear Son,

I am writing this at the beginning of the "empty nest" season of my life. The divorce rate is supposed to rise sixteen percent for parents nearing or during this stage. Claudia Arp wrote that in this season, husbands and wives "look around at the other bird in their nest and think they don't *know* them and they're not sure they *like* them and not sure they want to spend *another 30 years in the marriage*."

Another online article I read from a study in the U.K. found there was a noticeable rise in couples splitting up after forty or fifty years of marriage. The article said that one couple chose to separate at age ninety-two. I don't know about you, son, but I think if that was me I could hang in there, if for nothing else, for the sake of the kids!

I know that you witnessed our marriage as it went through a bit of a shaky stage these last few years. But I want you to know that we are coming out the other end of the tunnel and the fight for our marriage has been well worth it for both of us and also for *you*. Here are some quite revealing quotes:

> "Whether I'm 7 or 27, I'm still my parent's child and it's still my family that's breaking up."

> "It rips your whole world apart. Everything you thought you were sure of, suddenly you're not sure of."

"It was a terrible time. I went through all the pain and grief that any child does when this sort of thing happens, but I had the added bonus of having zero support because I was an adult."

You know, son, this tells me that if your mom and I were to divorce, that would be still be very hard for you to experience as an adult. That is one of the reasons I am so committed to remaining vigilant in working on my marriage now more than ever. I see that I can *never* be complacent in the marriage relationship. There is so much at stake for the next generation and beyond. Whenever I become tempted to complacency or hardness of heart, I think of you, son, your siblings and your nieces.

I am not being judgmental toward those who cannot make it the entire way; there are many reasons for marriages to break up. I get that. But for me, son, part of the legacy your mom and I want to leave to you is a lasting marriage. You will be richer for it. We want our family to know that we really did love each other and that marriage is to be for a lifetime, no matter what challenges you may face.

Son, I know I have been a far-from-perfect example to you in the way I have loved your mom. For these shortcomings I have many regrets. But I hope you have seen that I haven't given up, that I admit my weaknesses, acknowledge my sins, and keep pressing on.

I received an email from Adrian Hickmon, the founder of Capstone Treatment Center, in Arkansas. He was writing to fathers whose children had gone through his treatment center. This is what he wrote that encouraged me:

In my opinion, "humble authenticity" is the gift good fathers give by changing for the better. To honestly take a look at ourselves in the mirror includes hard crucibles,

God's mysterious ways, frustrations, injustices, difficulties, finally "putting the dots together," and more—then making sustained efforts to change for the better. This process must include owning our own mistakes, expressing remorse and regret, asking for forgiveness, and committing to do differently. It must be the most difficult aspect of human life, one reason it's such a special gift to our children.

Humbly offering you that "gift,"

Dad

Sometimes Commitment Just Isn't Enough

Dear Son,

I have walked alongside several men recently who have undergone divorce after they had done everything humanly possible to preserve their marriages, but to no avail. Tragically, their former wives did not share their commitment to fight for their marriage. Clearly it takes *both* partners to make a marriage work, no matter how committed one of them may be.

On another level, I have found that commitment isn't enough, son. I have learned to distrust my will power, my "commitment," to be sufficient strength to produce any lasting behavioral change in me. At seventeen, I discovered that I had been trying to live the life God desired of me in my own strength, in my own power. Because of my experiences through those efforts, I had falsely concluded that the Christian life just didn't work. But what I was living was not "Christianity" but "Ianity" (Christianity minus Christ). That sure doesn't work!

Getting back to the marriage issue, I don't know of anything better than marriage, because it has taught me that

I need to completely depend upon Christ to do something that I am unable to pull off in my own strength. For example, I can "commit" to love your mom as Christ loved the church, sacrificially and unconditionally. But as your sister, Heidi, would say, "Are you kidding me right now?"

Why am I telling you this? I just want you to know that marriage is going to put you into situations that are beyond your natural ability to handle. That is okay. In fact that is really good; marriage is one of God's choice instruments to develop your character into Christ-likeness. Don't run from marriage because of the trials you will face. I believe many in your generation have run from the commitment, as they have seen how hard it is to sustain. As Martin Luther was known to have said about the sanctifying power of marriage, "One year of marriage is worth ten in a monastery."

But I tell you, the lasting joys and qualities that will develop in you make the relatively small difficulties more than worth it! If you find yourself in a troubled marriage, I hope you won't try to escape it. I hope you will persevere through it. If your wife chooses to leave, then you will know that you have done your part. There is no shame in that.

I pray that doesn't happen to you, son. But if it does, God has lessons for you in that, too.

> We can't, but He can through us,
>
> Dad

I've Only Just Begun

Dear Son,

We live in a hyper-sexualized culture. It is obsessive. Sure, sex and romance are a legitimate and healthy part of marriage, but when sex is glorified as being all there is to marriage, then we can easily be deceived to believe that, well, that *is* all there is to marriage!

As your mom and I enter the empty nest season of our lives, and as I walk alongside men who are doing the same, I find that the over-emphasis upon sex and romance creates unrealistic expectations that neither husband nor wife can fulfill.

When your mom and I were married some three and a half decades ago (boy, do I look like a young geek in my wedding picture!) we adopted the Carpenters' song, *We've Only Just Begun,* as our marriage theme song. It was a great song that we interpreted to mean that no matter how long we are married, we will be able to say, "We've only just begun," because we have entered into a covenant with an Eternal Third Partner, the Lord Jesus Christ Himself.

But you know son, as I think about what marriage has taught me about God's love for your mom and me, I can honestly say, "I, not just we, have only just begun!" Every time I am called to love your mom and she is not able to reciprocate, every time I must try to understand, even if I am not understood, every time I seek to lead but am not followed, I get a taste of Christ's love for me. I'm not putting your mom down; it is simply the reality of a husband seeking to learn to love as Christ loves—without conditions.

Son, "I've only just begun" to learn of God's love that He poured out so lavishly upon me through the cross. "I've only just begun" to plumb the depths of His love that desires to be loved, but never demands it in return.

And son, isn't *that* the kind of love worth obsessing over!

Because His love is always new,

Dad

Chapter 4

Choose to Serve
(Not Just Observe)

*"Do all the good you can, by all the means you can, in all
the ways you can, to all the people you can, in all the places
you can, as long as you can."*

—John Wesley

Serving Is More Fun than Surfing

Dear Son,

Remember the Christmas trips to Mexico and later, the
Central America trips we made? We have some precious
family memories and some funny moments that live on in
Bohnett family lore. I won't embarrass you by retelling any
stories here. But while we remember those Christmases
well, we probably have a hard time remembering many of
those we had at home.

You probably wondered why your mom and I felt so
strongly about taking you and your siblings on different
short-term mission trips when you were younger. The
reason is simple: When I stepped out of my comfort zone

as a high school junior for the first time, I was able to understand Christ's love personally for me. Understanding moved from my head to my heart. I wanted the same thing to happen to you.

I remember that junior year spring break well. Since I lived in Hawaii, normally I would have spent my time surfing. But that year I decided to go with our church's youth singing group, "The New Life Singers," on a trip to Maui to help plant a new church. This involved things like passing out invitations door-to-door to perfect strangers. This was waaaaaaaay out of my comfort zone. If I could have gone AWOL I would have, but Oahu was a long way to swim from Maui! We read through a chapter in the book of Galatians each day. On the second day we read Galatians 2:20: "I have been crucified with Christ and I no longer live, but Christ lives in me. The life I live in the body, I live by faith in the Son of God, who loved me and gave himself for me."

After singing in shopping malls and in nightly concerts before our pastor preached, we saw several people come forward and give their hearts to Christ. That was a joy I had never experienced before. From that point on, I determined that I wanted to be involved with what God was doing; it was so much more exciting and fulfilling than what I was doing on my own in just seeking to fulfill my own needs.

I don't think I would have understood that verse unless I was put in a situation where I was in "over my head." That's what is great about serving others, like short-term missions. It puts us in that place. I encourage you to continue to do this as an adult. You will always receive more from it than you give. It is what I call being "sanctifiedly selfish." You will never regret it. I guarantee it!

Serving is more fun than surfing!

Dad

Lighting a Candle Beats Cursing the Darkness

Dear Son,

I remember when I was a kid, I used to watch a religious program occasionally on television (I think it was sponsored by the Lutheran church), which opened up with a person lighting a candle and the narrator saying, "It is better to light one candle than to curse the darkness." I really didn't get the symbolism they were using, but I thought the hand lighting a candle in a dark room was pretty cool.

I have never forgotten that little phrase, but I have forgotten to practice the message that the phrase conveyed. I have been focused a lot lately upon the growing darkness of our culture. It seems that no matter where I turn—television, radio, or the Internet—the darkness seems to be breaking in like a relentless flood. As a dad, I have worried about what kind of world you and your children would be living in.

You know, son, since I have a melancholy personality, it is not good for me to dwell too much on things like that. I know I will soon start sounding like just another "grumpy old man." Here's a verse that speaks to me: "Do everything without complaining or arguing, so that you may become blameless and pure, children of God without fault in a crooked and depraved generation, in which you shine like stars in the universe as you hold out the word of life" (Philippians 2:14-16a).

It seems to me, son, this whole thing comes down to perspective. We cannot really expect a culture that has rejected God to become anything but "crooked and depraved." And have we ever thought that in God's redemptive purposes, He has strategically placed His people to stand out in the darkness and point the way to Himself? In fact, when times are the darkest, light stands out all the more. That is exactly what happens in both the physical and spiritual realm.

You know, son, on one of those rare cloudless evenings in the Seattle area when you can see the stars clearly, the stars aren't that bright when compared to places on the other side of the Cascades away from the city lights. In those less populated areas, the artificial light from the ground doesn't obscure the magnificent display of the stars that shine to contrast the darkness. The darker the sky the more glorious these lights shine!

Things are tough in our nation now, son, but I remember a time that was also tumultuous when I was in my middle to late teens. Our country was in the midst of multiple convulsions because of a heated-up cold war, the Vietnam War, violent civil protests, social upheaval, the assassinations of RFK and MLK, racial unrest, a Middle East oil embargo, Watergate, growing inflation, and two Arab-Israeli wars. You get the picture.

But something else happened during that time that profoundly impacted your mother and me. It was called "The Jesus Movement." This was the largest ingathering of souls into the kingdom throughout North America in the twentieth century. When disillusionment over the things that my generation had previously believed began to set in, many turned to Christ.

It was the darkness of that time that made the light of Jesus shine so bright to meet our desperate needs. There were religious counterfeits, theological confusion, and those who fell away from simple faith in Christ, but that does not negate the genuine work of God during that period.

The Spirit of God led this movement. The leaders He raised up were those who recognized that the darkness that had befallen America was a fresh opportunity to present the light of Christ to our generation. They saw a vision of contrasting communities of light in the midst of an increasingly dark culture that would draw people to Jesus.

The word of God—the message of the gospel—was simply held out to searching people without any "political correctness." We were dubbed "Jesus Freaks" during that time in the same way the early Christ-followers were mockingly called "Christians" or "little Christs" in the first century.

Son, I believe that time of turmoil was not as great as what you and your children will experience. I don't say this to scare you, but to encourage you that I believe you will be one of those who God will raise up in your generation to hold forth His light of hope. You will do this by simply pointing people to Jesus through how you live and speak. Someone was once asked, "How many people have you led to Christ?" His response was, "All of them I hope. Where else would I lead them?" Remember that. "Greater is He who is in you than he who is in the world" (1 John 4:4 NASB).

It *is* better to light one candle than to curse the darkness. And you are one of God's choice candles.

> Confident in what God will do
> through you in your generation,
>
> Dad

Chapter 5

Take Risks and Reap the Rewards

"Faith is to believe what you do not yet see; the reward for this faith is to see what you believe."

—Augustine

When Your Grandpa Rolled the Dice

Dear Son,

My dad, your grandpa, was involved in starting a business in 1957 that one day became a national restaurant chain. He did this between the ages of thirty-five and forty-five, while I was three to thirteen years of age. I had a chance recently to ask him how it actually started, and the story is an excellent example of how there are times in our life when we just need to take a calculated risk in order to reap the potential rewards.

When I recently sat with your grandpa I asked him, "So how did you and Sam actually start Sambo's Restaurants? I have heard your story in general terms over the years.

Can you give me more details?" He proceeded to tell me a fascinating story.

He was thirty-five years old and had just returned from being recalled by the Marine Corps to fly in the Korean Conflict. He was shot down over there and, fortunately for all of us, he was rescued from the icy cold water, or else none of us would be here! Then, after being in restaurant equipment sales for a few years, strictly on commission, he finally started to make some money. He had just put away $5,000 in cash in a local Santa Barbara bank.

One of his restaurant equipment clients was a man named Sam Battistone, who, along with his wife, Ione, owned and operated Sammy's Grill. Dad spent time getting to know Sam by stopping in his restaurant from time to time. He admired the way that he and his wife ran their little restaurant.

My mother was pregnant with my sister, Vikki, and he was feeling a bit nervous that his whole income was fully dependent upon commission sales. He thought to himself, *As long as I'm healthy we'll be okay, but with four kids now if I became sick or unable to work, we would be in big financial trouble.*

At that time, Sam Battistone was talking with a group of about ten men to see if they would be interested in investing in a new restaurant with him at a location on the beach in Santa Barbara. He invited dad to come to a meeting as well.

On the drive back, Sam asked dad what he thought about the opportunity. He replied, "I'm not interested in going into business with these guys, but Sam, if you ever want to do something together, let me know."

About two months later Sam called back to ask Dad if he was still interested, as the group of ten had all dropped out of the picture. "How much are we talking about?" Dad asked. Sam replied, "I think we can do this for about ten grand. We each can put in $5,000."

Dad thought about the $5,000 he had in the bank. Without too much thought, he withdrew it and took the wad of cash over to Sam. In a sense, he bet his future on what he believed he saw in Sam as a businessman.

It was important to keep this arrangement secret for a while as your grandpa was still selling restaurant equipment, and he did not want this to be seen as a conflict of interest by other clients. As Sam came to the bank with your grandpa's cash the teller remarked to Sam that Newell Bohnett had just come in and withdrawn $5,000 in cash. Being quick on his feet, Sam's response was, "Ya, that Newell Bohnett is the worst poker player I've ever seen!"

That is how it all began, son. The restaurant adopted the Sambo's story, which would create a fun atmosphere with the murals for children to look at while eating their pancakes. They would later change their logo and murals in response to the Monterey chapter of the N.A.A.C.P. (National Association for the Advancement of Colored People). The new logo changed to a light-skinned turban-wearing Indian, from the African-looking Sambo character. The restaurant name, before political correctness of the late 1960s and '70s took hold in the U.S., seemed to be a perfect combination of the two men's names, "Sam" Battistone and Newell "Bo" Bohnett. Your grandpa was often called Bo by his friends.

Twenty years later that one little restaurant grew into a national chain of more than 1,000 restaurants, with more than 250,000 employees, and its stock was traded on the New York Stock Exchange. It continued until its eventual bankruptcy in 1984. Sam and my dad were able to retire in 1968; your grandpa was only forty-five years old.

Why do I tell you this story? Because I believe you have your own "Sambo's story" to live out. No, I don't think you are going to found a national restaurant chain like your grandpa did, but there is so much potential to start with something small and see it multiply and grow beyond your wildest dreams. It takes willingness to risk, as your grandpa did. He didn't start this until he was thirty-five, but all that he had gone through up to that time prepared him well when the opportunity came. He learned what he could from the difficult challenges of being in the Marine Corps and surviving two wars. He worked his best at his father's cabinet shop and later as a salesman living off commissions. The leaner times of his twenties and early thirties prepared and seasoned him for the opportunity that presented itself at thirty-five.

As you look to the Lord, son, know that he will not waste any of your work experiences. He will use them all to prepare you for the thing that *you* were created to do. As He was with your grandpa, and as He has been with me, He will be with you, son. When the time is right don't be afraid to take a risk. To risk and fail is not failure. Failure is to fail to risk.

> Believing in the multiplying impact
> of your life,
>
> Dad

My Father's Rescue from Above

Dear Son,

As a young boy I was always curious about what my dad did in World War II. He was a decorated Marine Corps pilot fighting in the Philippines, and was later recalled to fly in the Korean War. He fought in the Philippines as a young single man who had memorized the color-blindness test so he could be accepted in the Marine Corps flight program.

(I'm color blind too; it is a hereditary thing. Lucky you that you aren't).

He tried unsuccessfully to do all he could to avoid the Korean War as a married father of two, but to no avail. He smoked two packs of cigarettes and guzzled down several cups of coffee before the blood pressure test, as well as confessing that he had cheated on his color blindness test in the previous war.

As a child I thought I was alone in wanting my dad to talk to me about his war exploits and was frustrated by not being able to learn anything. It was not until I realized that this was a common response from most of that generation of war heroes. I was reminded of that recently when I reconnected with a high school classmate who had a very similar experience with his dad. Perhaps their way of coping with the pain of the war was to simply try to bury the memory of what they endured.

As a young boy, I remember asking Dad, "Did you ever kill anyone in the war?" or "Were you close enough to see the enemy when you were bombing?" Those questions were usually answered, "No," and if I followed up with, "What did you bomb then?" he would impatiently answer, "Rice paddies."

Disappointed, I walked away and thought to myself, *Great, Uncle Joe got shot in the stomach while fighting a bunch of Germans in hand-to-hand-combat at the Battle of the Bulge, and my dad killed rice from the air!*

As your grandpa is now well into his eighties, he is now more willing to talk about the war. So here's a story, son, that Grandpa told me that made me proud and grateful.

The Japanese Imperial Army had brutalized the Filipino people while occupying their islands, and had been very cruel captors of American prisoners. Dad was part of the American effort to drive the enemy out of the Philippines.

The Americans had received intelligence that the Japanese were executing American prisoners before they abandoned the prisons. They knew the location of one such prison where the Japanese still held Americans captive.

His mission was to bomb the walls in this prison, which would also eliminate the machine guns placed upon the walls facing inward. This would make possible a way of escape for the prisoners. To destroy the walls with gun emplacements would be a "twofer." The advantage of a dive bomb attack is they could come in somewhat unexpectedly from the air, fairly accurately drop a bomb and then "hopefully" pull up in time to escape enemy fire, which was easier said than done.

He said, "It was just like in the movies. I dropped down on them, dropped the bomb, and as I pulled up to look back I could see those little guys flying up in the air as the walls collapsed. My tail gunner was so excited by the direct hit that he almost shot the tail off our plane as I jerked it abruptly upward."

Why this story stirred me was because I could imagine myself as one of those frightened, starving POWs, knowing that my life would be taken at any moment by my vengeful, fleeing captors. For a moment I could taste a little of what they must have felt when they saw one of our planes take out in one fell swoop those machine guns stationed on the walls that were holding them captive. Grandpa provided deliverance from certain doom with one well-placed bomb!

And this is a little bit of a picture of what Jesus did for us, son. He came from above, not as a roaring plane laden with guns and bombs, but as a baby in a manger, and later as a grown man dying on a cross. We were hopelessly and helplessly captive awaiting certain death, until He came down from above. With His death on the cross and resurrection from the grave, He shattered the walls and destroyed the weapons that held us in a state of a living death forever.

I know the analogy is flawed, but just the same, as I think about your grandpa's bombing mission that day decades ago in the Philippines, I gain a new dimension of gratitude for our heavenly Father's divinely conceived rescue from above for you and for me!

> Forever grateful for our heavenly
> Father's rescue from above,
>
> Dad

My Decision to Invest My Life in the Unseen

Dear Son,

I have never explained to you what I believe my "calling" is. I know you have heard about my conversion at age seventeen, but I don't think you've heard about the shift in my life that happened when I was twenty years old.

As you know, your grandpa cast a pretty big shadow over my life. When I was eighteen and he was in "retirement," he bought PuuWaaWaa Ranch on the Big Island of Hawaii, which was the second largest ranch in the state, next to the Parker Ranch. To me, it looked like my future would be there—and I loved it! After graduating from high school, I worked that summer at the ranch. The only college I considered going to was Hilo College, because it was on the other side of the Big Island and that is where I wanted to be.

But there was one problem: Your mom was not on that island and I was in love! As my first semester of college went along, I became more frustrated about not being able to be with her. At Christmas break I decided that I didn't want to go back to Hilo College, but I wanted to transfer to the University of Hawaii, Manoa, to be closer to her. However, by the time I figured that out, it was too late. What was I going to do now?

Well, our church had just begun a tiny Bible college, called International College. I loved Pastor Jim and the way he would strongly challenge us as young people to live our lives for God, but I never saw myself going to a Bible college, because that was mainly a school for missionaries and pastors, and that surely wasn't me. One thing I thought of as I considered going to International College was, *"If I just go for one year, I will have one year of Bible, and no matter what, that will never be wasted."* So I took a calculated risk and began to attend.

That semester was such a contrast to my first semester at Hilo College. I had boomeranged back to living at home. One main benefit was that I became much healthier by eating your grandmother's delicious home cooking. I was able to see Cindy much more frequently as she was now a senior in high school nearby. As I took classes at International Bible College something began to stir in me. As I studied the Bible the bigness of God and who He is began to impact me.

In April of that year, your mom and I spent all night on the phone talking about getting married! That spring break she came to the ranch and it was there, on top of PuuWaaWaa's cinder cone hill that I asked her to marry me, after I had received her father's permission.

I worked on the ranch again that summer and we were married on April 3, 1974. After working on the ranch a little more, we moved to Oahu and rented a cute little house overlooking Kaneohe Bay from your grandmother that was just a couple of blocks from where my parents lived. I continued my school that fall, and your mom joined me for some classes. Soon after, all the students from the college went on a retreat to Camp Timberline.

Timberline was a magical place for me. That is where I had really "seen" Cindy for the first time, driving up to the camp a couple of years before. I had to pinch myself in disbelief that this beautiful blue-eyed blonde would ever pay attention to me! It was only later that I learned that your grandpa was instrumental in the church being able to purchase that camp property.

So we were back at Camp Timberline. Pastor Jim, who was also the president of the college, preached messages to us that asked the question, "What are you going to give your life to?" Until that time the biggest thing I could think of was that wonderful ranch that had become "a family affair." The table was set for me there. What could be more exciting, more fun, more fulfilling than having a life in a place like that on the Big Island of Hawaii?

But the messages I heard at Camp Timberline changed everything. Suddenly the ranch and all of its appeal could not compete with the idea of investing my life in spreading the gospel. I didn't know what that would mean, but I wanted in. I had tasted enough of being part of building His kingdom that I knew that serving God gave me a joy that no place on earth could provide. In my mind I was also able to project myself into old age and think about this crossroads where I now stood. What if I hardened my heart to this call? What regrets would I have? What sorrow would I feel? I knew what I wanted to give my life to. I wasn't sure about the details, but I determined that God's purpose was going to be my purpose—whatever that looked like.

This purpose was confirmed in the next three years at International Bible College, and I heard the message very clearly that Jesus gave to Simon Peter in John 21 when He said, "Feed my sheep." I know I have not been a pastor in a traditional sense, but as I look back on my journey, no matter what job I had or career path I took, my "calling" has been one of shepherding people. This has just come out of me. Sometimes this has been a delight and other times it has been a challenge, but always it has been God's clear call on my life.

I wanted you to know this, because without this knowledge you can't really know my heart or understand the choices that your mom and I have made in our lives. None of what you know about me would make much sense if you don't understand my calling to live for the unseen and the eternal.

With no regrets so far,

Dad

Chapter 6

Have the Courage to Go Against the Flow

"Don't do what others will do or can do when there is so much that others will not do or cannot do."
—Dawson Trotman

A Worm's Head Can Turn Out to Be a Snake's Tail

Dear Son,

Do you remember what I wrote about my being called to be a shepherd? This calling was severely tested when we were at the church where you grew up as a young Christian. There was a sense of excitement and vibrancy at that church, and there were so many very good people there. Your mom and I prayed about becoming members since it appeared to be so dedicated to reaching out to non-believers and establishing new believers. We could see this was a perfect fit with our call to shepherd others. We were excited to join this dynamic young church!

Sometime later, I was asked to become an elder. I was happy to serve. I won't get into details because it really isn't necessary and you already know most of them. Needless to say, the pastor wasn't the man he professed to be. The next two years were painful and tumultuous, and I was at the center of the storm that raged. I knew things that I couldn't reveal the facts about to those in the congregation, but I found myself judged by those who didn't know the full story and couldn't know the full story. It was greatly frustrating because I wanted to look good in the eyes of others, which you know to be a weakness of mine, but instead I was being called to stand strong and do the right thing.

I wanted to quit many times in the middle of these struggles. But I knew that I couldn't. I needed to finish the course I was on. I felt that there were so many wounded people counting on me, and I wanted to be found faithful by the Lord. The church eventually dwindled down to a very small number and then merged with another. I had longings to see it prosper stronger than ever, but that never happened. I wasn't called to be a dynamic pastoral leader. The former pastor who wounded so many people was a far more gifted and effective leader than I could ever be. That wasn't my call. I was called to be a shepherd and to care for the sheep. I did my best until I felt released of my commitment.

As you know, we then moved on to another church, because I believed that the circumstances of that trauma had already stolen enough from our family. As you think of that experience, I hope you will not be bitter or cynical about church leadership. There are many good pastors out there. This man just wasn't who we all thought he was. He had a dark side that finally overpowered the good and the giftedness that we had all seen in him.

I also hope you realize that my commitment to stand up for those who had been victimized by him was something I did first of all for the Lord, who called me to care for His sheep, second for the victims and their families, but also for *you*. I wanted to leave a legacy of courage that you could build on. I drew from the courage of my dad, knowing I came from a courageous heritage. Yes, your grandpa had great courage in World War II and Korea, but I also saw him go through the pain of watching the restaurant chain that he had so carefully built being destroyed. He had to go against the flow and fight, even though it was to no avail. No doubt there will be times in your life when you will be in similar situations, when you will be dealing with more than you have bargained for.

When I was going through the church crisis, I remember I got this picture in my mind. It was of a bird trying to pull a worm from out of the ground. The only problem was the bird didn't have the head of a worm in his mouth but rather the tail of a giant snake burrowed into the earth! That is what happens sometimes. We don't know the battle against incredible evil that we face until we have already committed ourselves to the fight! Your grandpa often quoted: "When we are up to our a** in alligators, it is hard to remember why we decided to drain the swamp in the first place!"

I didn't handle myself perfectly by any means in that church leadership situation, and I did make some mistakes, but one thing I will never regret: By God's grace He gave me the courage to go against the flow! You *will* be tested as well, son, it is just a matter of time. Here is a proverb I thought of often in that situation. "Like a muddied spring or a polluted well is a righteous man who gives way to the wicked" (Proverbs 25:26).

We Can Stand In *His* strength,

Dad

Relevant or Reverent?

Dear Son,

You know my book, that best-selling hit that has rocked the publishing world, "Like Father, Like Son"? Not! Well it was an eye-opening experience for me concerning the Christian publishing world. Like the church leadership experience, son, it is not about the sin "out there," but about the sin in me, that is drawn and enticed by the very thing that I despise!

I can remember waiting for my designated book-signing time one afternoon at the Christian Bookseller's Convention in Denver. I used much of the time at the convention to network with people who I thought might be interested in my book about fathering. But something else happened to me as I walked through aisle after aisle of booths promoting religious books, gifts, and paraphernalia. After awhile this whole scene just started to weird me out!

It was truly bizarre. The first thing I was greeted with was "Christian pirates" (isn't that a bit of an oxymoron?) crying, "Arrrr, matey. Praise the Lord!" This no doubt was timed to capitalize on the "Pirates of the Caribbean" craze that was going on at the time. Then there were clowns on stilts and Jesus candy called "Testamints," and creepy looking Jesus dolls (think "Chucky" with a beard). You get the picture.

I noticed that the books that were big sellers seemed to be all about relevance and *not* reverence. I started to think that maybe the saying was true about the church after all, that the church is like a pool, and all of the noise seems to be coming from the shallow end. It all seemed so market-driven and not Spirit-led or Christ-centered. It was "Gospel Lite: tastes great, less filling."

When I talk about these things, I do not mean to point a condemning finger at my fellow Christians at that

41

convention. I was only peering into a mirror that reflected my own desire back to me to be relevant, my desire to gain an audience, to be popular and well received. But even as many of us have desired acceptance, success, and to make an impact in our world, gaining what we have defined as relevance, we have forgotten the whole concept of reverence.

I can't do anything about the past, but let me tell you where I am heading, son. I am pointing my life toward reverence. I believe that when you were a teen, you often may have thought I was pretty irrelevant anyway. Maybe now that you are older, you can begin to see me a bit differently. In any case, I know the best way for me to be relevant to you is to focus on my reverence toward the Lord. I will hopefully be a stepping-stone for your spiritual journey in these turbulent, man-glorifying waters we live in today.

> With reverence for the One who is
> eternally relevant,
>
> Dad

Temporal Failure or Eternal Success?

Dear Son,

As you know, your mom and I were involved in parenting ministry for several years of your childhood. We really had the best of motives, and I think that you and your siblings benefited from the sound, biblical approach to parenting we followed, even if it wasn't always perfectly applied.

But there was a subtle error that we believed and taught, though it is painful to admit now. The error, as simple as I can put it, is this: If parents raise their children "right" according to a set of biblical principles, prescribed teachings, and proven practices, then they are guaranteed to see them become committed Christian adults.

I do believe that chances improve for our children to embrace our faith and become "successful" adults when we follow biblical principles and practices as parents, but I don't think there is any guarantee. The trouble that I have found, son, with this "guaranteed success" kind of parenting mindset" is that it creates a "double bind" for the parents. Who will get the credit and the glory if we happen to "succeed" with a child or two? We say God, but secretly think it was our doing because we were smart enough or disciplined enough to rightly apply His recipe for successful parenting. We did it right. Our children are living proof! Can you smell the pride?

On the other hand, rather than feeling compassion and concern, we judge when we see children struggle as a result of making foolish choices or when there is rebellion. We look down our nose at that family and sigh, "We could see that coming." What this creates is a contagious disease of loneliness, gossip, shame, and guilt in the Christian "community."

Here is the paradox, son, that I have found and I know you must find in your own way: In order to "succeed" as a Christian, we often must "fail." For some, the failure will be subtle and almost imperceptible to outside observers. For others it will be *big* and dramatic. But I believe some failure is absolutely necessary in order for each of us to seek Christ out of real desperation. I believe, son, that Christ will not be all we *want* until He is all we *have*. Temporal failure creates the hunger for a success that is eternal.

You will no doubt have your own story of rescue in order for Jesus to be the "star" of the story. The test comes before the testimony. We each must come to that place where He is *our* Savior, *our* Rescuer—where Jesus is the star of *our* stories, no matter what failures or setbacks we experience.

Check out 2 Corinthians 1:3-4, and hopefully you will see that real *success* comes when our stories can be used to inspire others about this grace and power that is shown most through our weakness.

Often perplexed by this paradox,

Dad

Chapter 7

Dads Do Make
a Difference

"When I was a boy of fourteen, my father was so ignorant I could hardly stand to have the old man around. But when I got to be twenty-one, I was astonished at how much he had learned in seven years."

—Mark Twain

Bonds vs. Griffey

Dear Son,

As you may recall, we moved to the Seattle area at the very beginning of Ken "The Kid" Griffey Jr.'s baseball career. I watched you and your brother grow up idolizing him. His major league career inevitably came to an end two decades later.

You remember how Ken Griffey Jr. played when he was in his prime. He played the game with a seeming effortlessness that was amazing to watch. He was truly "The Natural." Whether he was chasing down a fly ball to the center field wall, throwing a base runner out, smacking another home run, or stealing a base, Ken Griffey Jr. seemed to do it all with boundless joy.

However, in these last two years, back with his original team, The Seattle Mariners, Griffey's age, injuries, and surgeries sharply eroded his baseball skills. His decision to retire was preceded by this once proud superstar sitting on the bench.

There is no doubt in anyone's mind that he will be remembered as one of the very best who ever played the game of baseball. Griffey's retirement reminds me of another player, Barry Bonds, who also recently retired. Bonds extended his record-breaking career well into his forties, eclipsing the single season home run record of Mark McGwire and the career home run record of Hank Aaron.

Both of these men had fathers who had All-Star major league careers, Ken Griffey Sr. and Bobby Bonds. And both of the sons surpassed their fathers' baseball greatness. Yet, Barry, Bobby's son, retired under a huge cloud of suspicion that he was using steroids illegally to enhance his performance. Ken Griffey Jr. retires now with what appears to be a clear record and great appreciation for what he accomplished without the help of banned steroids.

Barry's relationship with his father by his own account was distant. "I was a momma's boy. I didn't get anything from my dad, except my body and my baseball knowledge. The only time I spent with him was at the ballpark." His father, Bobby, died at age fifty-seven of lung cancer and a brain tumor.

On the other hand, Junior's relationship with his dad was close. "He's not only a great player," Griffey Jr. said of his dad in 1990, when he played alongside of him in the Seattle Mariner's outfield, "He's a great guy." I myself can remember twenty years ago watching them playing together in the outfield and watching them hit back-to-back singles at home and then back-to-back homers on the road. You could tell they really enjoyed being out there together.

In Jeff Pearlman's book about Barry Bonds titled *Love Me, Hate Me*, he records a very telling 1998 dinner conversation between Barry and Ken Griffey Jr. that I believe reveals why the legacies of these two great ball players will be so different. Barry is quoted as saying to Ken Griffey Jr., "As much as I've complained about McGwire and Canseco and all the bull with steroids, I'm tired of fighting it. I turn thirty-five this year. I've got three or four seasons left and I wanna get paid. I'm gonna start using some hard-core stuff, and hopefully it won't hurt my body. Then I'll get out of the game and be done with it."

Griffey reflected on that dinner conversation to Pearlman, "If I can't do it myself, then I'm not going to do it. When I'm retired, I want to at least be able to say, 'There's no question in our minds that he did it the right way.' I have kids. I don't want them to think their dad's a cheat."

There it is. One man was thinking selfishly of his own immediate benefit and the other had others on his mind, as well as his long-term legacy. One was thinking about the money and what it would bring him, and the other of what money can't buy, the respect of his children.

What do you think, son, made the difference between these two incredibly gifted athletes? The difference, I believe, was in the fathering they received. Bobby was a distant dad and Ken Sr. was a committed father who overcame a difficult relationship with his own father, Buddy, to tune into the hearts of both of his sons, Ken Jr. and Craig.

Someday, Lord willing, you will be a dad. I believe one of the benefits of being a dad is that it helps us to see our selfishness, then, if we are willing, to look past ourselves and think of the next generation. Because Ken Griffey Jr. had committed fatherhood modeled to him by his dad, he naturally thought in that way when he was tempted to make a selfish mistake. He was able to resist going down the steroids path that promised the "gold" of riches, fame, and broken records. Today that "gold" is clearly seen for what it is—fool's gold.

Son, this is "Father Power." I see you as a great dad someday with the ability to impact generations for the good. Don't underestimate the power you will be given. Bobby Bonds is still speaking through his son's choices and so is Ken Sr. through Junior's choices.

> Believing you are more like Griffey than Bonds,
>
> Dad

Lasting Snow

Dear Son,

Let me share another father-son baseball story that I read about a few years ago. This is the story of J.T. Snow, who the Red Sox acquired in a trade from the San Francisco Giants. J.T. is the son of Jack Snow, the former All-Pro wide receiver for the Los Angeles Rams from 1965 to 1975. I can tell you, son, as a former L.A. Rams fan those three words "complete to Snow" were music to my ears. Sadly, but with pride I'm sure, before Jack Snow passed away this January at sixty-two, J.T. told his dad that he would be wearing Jack's old number with the Rams, #84, when he plays for the Red Sox.

The father-son relationship had not been an easy one for J.T. and his siblings. Jack was a stern disciplinarian to J.T. and his sisters while they grew up, and he was often hyper critical and overbearing. J.T., though athletically gifted as his dad, inherited more of his mom's sensitive nature. There came a time just a few years ago when J.T. was playing baseball for the California Angels that he had not talked to his parents for two and a half years. Even when he learned that his mother had cancer, the silence continued.

But the story doesn't end there. Of course you remember ol' Randy Johnson. He would never be accused of being a "touchy feely" kind of guy. Well, in a spring training game in 1997, a 100-mph Johnson fastball hit J.T.'s wrist and ricocheted to hit the orbital bone around his left eye. It was then that J.T. called his parents and they took the call.

As he recovered from the accident, the relationship with his parents went through a healing as well. His mother died that following year of breast cancer. J.T. and his wife named their son, who was born eight months after her death, "Shane" to honor her, as Shane was her maiden name.

In the precious few years that followed, Jack, J.T., and Shane formed a special three-generational bond. The love the three had for one another was evident to all who saw them together. The Giant's equipment manager nicknamed the three Snows, "Snow Man" (Jack), "Snow Ball" (J.T.) and "Snow Flake" (Shane).

Jack passed away in 2006. But because of J.T.'s choice, and with a little help from a Randy Johnson fastball, he finally reconnected with his father and made this story a happy one. He chose to forgive whatever wrongs he felt he suffered from his dad, and he honored his parents with gratitude and acceptance. Because of that, Shane has a legacy of having known his grandfather and seeing his dad love and honor him.

Son, I know that I didn't do it all right as your dad. I pray we never get to a place where we are not talking to each other. If we ever hit such an impasse, I pray that it won't be for long. Life is too short for that. In the long run, what is important are the relationships we have. They are worth much more than our accomplishments. You know that I am a baseball fan, but I couldn't tell you how much longer

J.T.'s career lasted after 2006. Yet I can tell you that he has honored his dad, Jack, and loved his son, Shane, and that makes him a Hall of Famer in my book!

Longing for a lasting legacy,

Dad

Cutting Wood and Building "Bridges"

Dear Son,

I have been involved with mentoring dads for several years, as you know. I have a friend who lives in Monroe, Washington, with whom I meet in a town nearby for breakfast once a month for mutual support on our fathering journeys. Over the past several years, this man faithfully supported our ministry to fathers with the hard-earned profits from his construction business.

As we have watched our young adults begin to leave home and find their way, we have both been perplexed that this "launching" has not been as easy as we had envisioned. My friend has three sons and each has taken a different road entering the adult world. He had begun to experience some depression as his sons struggled. He thought that he had failed as a father even though, in my opinion, he had been extremely faithful. Together he and his wife had home-schooled their older sons and younger daughters and raised them in an active, Bible-believing church.

During one of our breakfast times, he began to talk about one of his sons who had joined the Army and was engaged to be married. Recently his son, who could only spend one day at home before he needed to return from a military leave, surprised him with what he wanted to do on that one precious day. "I want to spend it with you, Dad, cutting and stacking wood together, just like we used to do," his son said to him. My friend's voice cracked a bit when he talked about him.

His son then explained to his dad that in the Army he was often asked how he learned to do so many things. He would smile and explain, "Let me tell you about a boy who grew up with his dad in the woods."

My friend thought that much of his "hands-on" fathering had been wasted, but now he was hearing that he had not only equipped his son with a certain amount of practical competence as a young adult, but he had created father-son memories that his son deeply valued. My breakfast buddy is now convinced that he wasn't just cutting wood with his son; he was *building a "bridge."*

When you become a dad, whatever you enjoy doing, share it with your sons and daughters! They will be forever grateful.

Treasuring our memories we created,

Dad

A Father's Blessing to His Children: Why the Resistance?

Dear Son,

A few years ago I watched the film, "Flags Of Our Fathers" with your grandpa, who is a veteran of both World War II and the Korean War. He said that the film disappointed him. He felt the controversy about the photograph of the flag-raising over Mt. Surabachi distracted the audience from what was actually accomplished by the Marines at Iwo Jima. I can see his point. However, what left the most lasting impression on me after seeing this film was how determined both sides were, the Americans and the Japanese, in controlling this seemingly insignificant little rock of an island way out in the Pacific Ocean.

Coincidentally, the morning after watching this film I attended a class I was co-teaching with another father in which we were instructing men how to write letters of blessing to their children. As we talked about how the previous week's assignment had gone, I was surprised by the amount of internal opposition the men were experiencing in doing this seemingly simple task. I thought, *Why the resistance?*

Then my mind went back to "Flags of Our Fathers" and the battle of Iwo Jima. Both the Japanese and the Americans realized that Mt. Surabachi was the key to controlling the island of Iwo Jima, and Iwo Jima was extremely important for the American advance to Japan itself. Once under U.S. control, an air base could be built that would enable air raids to be launched directly against Japan.

The identity of Iwo Jima was transformed from a Japanese stronghold to an American launching pad through a very bloody and costly battle. The intensity of the enemy's resistance and the Marines' efforts were in direct proportion to what was at stake for both sides. To me this illustrates why it is so difficult for us as men to follow through to give destiny-affirming blessings to our families. Our enemy, the devil, knows power of those blessings and how it will project deeply into his territory through the generations.

The intensity of the enemy's resistance is in direct proportion to what is at stake for both the kingdom of light and the kingdom of darkness in the battle for the hearts of family members.

So, son, I want you to know that you are *my* son whom I love and with you I am well pleased. I know I have said it to you before, but I just don't ever want you to forget it. You have my blessing; now launch out with confidence that you are highly valued, esteemed, and treasured by your dad, and as you move forward, you can carry that blessing to your future wife, children, and grandchildren.

Because generations are at stake,

Dad

Uncle Clem: A Father to the Fatherless

Dear Son,

Let me share just one more "Father Power" story that shows that you can be a powerful father, even if you are not one biologically. This is about Clem Wehe who passed away in 2008 at ninety years of age. I first met "Uncle Clem" in the summer of 1971 when he was courting (yes, old-fashioned courting!) my widowed Aunt Sheila, who was the mother of thirteen children (actually fourteen, but one died of a congenital heart defect as an infant) in Santa Barbara, California. Uncle Clem was a brother in the Franciscan Order and had known her family through working with the Bohnett boys when they attended St. Anthony's Seminary.

In June of 1972, Uncle Clem, a single man in his mid-fifties, suddenly became a father to those thirteen Bohnett children when he married Sheila. What amazed me about Uncle Clem was the way he continued to honor the memory of my Uncle Joe to all of the kids. He never tried to compete with Joe's memory, but he encouraged stories to be told about their father.

One fact I did not know about Uncle Clem was that he, like Uncle Joe, had been awarded both a Bronze Star medal and a Purple Heart medal for bravery while fighting the Nazis in Europe. Though he had been a warrior, he had serenity about him, an ability to be a calming influence to all others in the room. His life motto was taken from St. Francis: "Lord, make me an instrument of your peace." For sure, that trait of peacemaking was a valuable asset to bring into the family of thirteen children when he married Sheila, with several of them highly energetic teenagers!

Both Uncle Clem and Aunt Sheila, who passed away from cancer in 2003, were strong Christians. Their home was directly across from their Catholic church in Santa Barbara. Though Uncle Clem was considered a "brother" in the Franciscan Order and a "step-father" technically to the Bohnett children, he was a *real* father who imparted quiet, godly strength to this family.

Remember, true fatherhood is more than biological.

Thanking God for Uncle Clem's example,

Dad

Chapter 8

With a Little Help from Our Friends

"The only way to have a friend is to be one."
—Ralph Waldo Emerson

Something's Gotta Die

Dear Son,

A while back I attended a men's retreat where we were entertained by a cowboy cook named Cookie. This guy cooks for hunting and fishing trips, and is big enough to be two men! His comment about our first retreat breakfast, consisting mostly of fruits and grains, was, "That wasn't a meal. That's what food eats. To make a real meal, *something's gotta die!*"

Those words were the most memorable ones spoken at that retreat.

Son, as I have reflected upon the words of that cowboy philosopher, I realize this idea has much to say to us as men. When it comes to being a man who can walk in true fellowship with other men, something that we are commanded by Christ to do, something needs to die.

You have probably experienced going to church or being in some gathering with professing Christians, when you realize it is not a safe place to show weakness or vulnerability. We feel almost compelled to yield to the pressure to portray an image of having it all together. What needs to die is that image. To keep that mask on may help us feel better in one way, but we still walk away burdened, discouraged, and alone.

To be willing to be open and honest with another man, a friend, a brother in Christ, I have to "die" to my false belief that it is better to portray to others an image of success or competency than to be honest with a few trusted friends. For me, son, this has meant I had to sometimes humble myself before another guy to admit a weakness, failure, or helplessness to change a harmful habit. This is hard because it isn't modeled very much in our culture today.

The wonderful thing is this "death" is not the end of the story. There is a resurrection that follows when we dare to be open about our struggles and weaknesses. This is where Christ shows His sufficiency like no other way. As someone has wisely said, "Jesus likes to hang out at the end of ropes."

Son, I can't emphasize this enough. Find a handful of trusted friends. You may need to start with just one. That is fine. But be real with that friend. It will be much more helpful if this is a praying friend. There is an extra element of power at work in that case. James 5:16 says, "Therefore confess your sins to each other and pray for each other so that you may be healed. The prayer of a righteous man is powerful and effective."

Because we need lifetime friends,

Dad

The Importance of Family Friends

Dear Son,

I am sure that you remember growing up in Redmond, Washington, near the Barshaw family. The five years they lived nearby was a gift. They have been family friends for some thirty years now. I pray when God gives you a godly wife and Lord willing, you are blessed with children, that He brings at least one family to journey alongside you.

You remember that Christmas when Pastor Brad decided that he wanted to give us that very first Christmas experience, and we put hay in their garage and we all slept out in below 20-degree weather on Christmas eve on the cold concrete. I had a sore throat for a week after that, but to this day we still talk about it.

You also remember the camping trip we took with them to Lake Curlew. Unfortunately, we only did this once, but it was a lifetime memory. I remember that squirrel that kept throwing pinecones on us as we were eating at the picnic table below "his tree."

Family life is tough with many unexpected twists and turns. To have good friends walk with us can make all the difference in the world. Isn't it great to have Pastor Brad and Auntie Nita, Jana, Julie, and Jon who love and accept you as you are? To have family friends like these is worth asking God for and worth fighting to keep, even if you hit rough spots in the road along the way.

Grateful for lasting friendships,

Dad

We Need Battle Buddies

Dear Son,

I know you have heard this before, but it's worth repeating. We are in a war. This is a life and death battle for the future of our very souls and the souls of others. Eternal destinies are at stake. This isn't a game.

Let me tell you why I feel so strongly about the importance of the small group for our spiritual health. Many Christian men don't see the value of the small group. The enemy will do all he can to keep us as men away from a genuine Bible-saturated, life sharing, praying group of men who are committed to follow Jesus and love one another in this broken world.

There are certain periods we go through when we are more acutely aware of the reality and extent of the battle. I know there are many times of challenge I would have never made it through without my "battle buddies." Someone has said, "Throughout life we are plagued by inexperience." We need our wiser, older brothers *and* our exuberant, younger brothers to fight alongside of us.

It really doesn't have to be that complicated. Acts 2:42 lays it out for us: "They devoted themselves to the apostles' teaching and to the fellowship, to the breaking of bread and to prayer." That's it. When men do these four things in a balanced format, something transformational occurs. Just reading God's word together as we share our lives and pray for each other is life changing.

The more I read the Bible, the more I see that this is what is on God's heart: His Son and His people. Only two things on this earth last for eternity: the word of God and people. This is what I want to give my life to. How about you?

Thankful for my battle buddies,

Dad

Chapter 9

Practice the Attitude of Gratitude

"A life in thankfulness releases the glory of God."
—Bengt Sundberg

Gratitude that Leads to Fervency

Dear Son,

I think the most important thing that I have learned through my marriage to your mother is this: I have found that I have a natural tendency to gravitate toward an attitude of "entitlement." I often look at the relationship through the grid of what I deserve rather than what I need to be giving. I have found that if I do not guard my heart from this attitude, then it will always lead me to complacency, which is passive, lazy inactivity. This is so dangerous because I usually am not even aware that I have slipped into this entitlement/complacency syndrome. It usually takes some painful discipline from our gracious heavenly Father to wake me up.

Psalm 119:67, 71 I Peter 1:22, 2 Cor. 5:15 has been helpful in that regard: "Before I was afflicted I went astray, but now I obey your word...It was good for me to be afflicted, so that I might learn your decrees."

The antidote for this problem is to have an attitude of gratitude, which is the opposite of entitlement. I find that when I become grateful again for my wife and start expressing it to her, it takes my eyes off of what she isn't doing for me. I then get them onto Christ and what He has done for me. The more I look to Him, the more complacency is replaced with fervent passion to love my wife again.

The Scriptures speak to this:

> Now that you have purified yourselves by obeying the truth so that you have sincere love for your brothers, love one another deeply, from the heart.
>
> —1 Peter 1:22

> And he died for all, that those who live should no longer live for themselves but for him who died for them and was raised again.
>
> —2 Corinthians 5:15

Christ must be the source of love in marriage, son. No matter how great your wife is, and I am believing that you *will* have a wonderful wife, she cannot be your primary "source"; only Jesus can be that for you.

Grateful that He first loved us,

Dad

An Attitude of Gratitude

Dear Son,

I have told you how we just naturally gravitate toward this attitude of entitlement when it comes to what we feel we deserve from people, groups, or God. And you have watched me have my ups and downs in my relationship with your mom. Let me tell you again that most of the problems came out of a spirit of entitlement that I held in the relationship. I told myself, "I deserve to be treated this way or spoken to that way, or responded to in the way I wanted to be responded to." When my expectations were not fulfilled, I found myself saying or doing hurtful things in retaliation. Then the spiral continued until there was forgiveness asked for and granted. I honestly don't know how couples ever survive who cannot regularly humble themselves before each other, ask to be forgiven, and forgive each other!

I know this isn't anything really new to you, but I want you to consider this very carefully. An "*attitude* of gratitude" is one important characteristic that I am working on developing in my own life, and I hope you see its importance for your own. Without consciously working on this, in our sinfulness, we will naturally gravitate toward an entitlement mindset, which leads to complacency and laziness in our relationships. As I said before, what makes this so dangerous, I believe, is that we are usually not even aware when we have fallen into this way of thinking.

And as I said earlier, the antidote to this entitlement/ complacency problem is simply to put our eyes onto Christ and what He has done in our behalf. Once this occurs, we can begin to cultivate an *attitude* of gratitude, which is then translated into a new sense of urgency in loving the people that we are called to love, whether that be our spouse, child, friend, or co-worker.

61

I know you know this is easier said than done. To live this way forces us to swim against the cultural tide. Don't get down on yourself when you find that you have slipped in your gratitude. Just get back on the horse. Make daily thanksgiving a discipline even when you don't feel like it. One thing I have done most mornings is to reflect upon what God has done in my life in the past twenty-four hours. That helps me because I realize that it is so easy to overlook the "small blessings"; even though the Lord gives them to me on a daily basis, I tend to easily forget them.

For example, here is a sample of my twenty-four hour list on this random fall, rainy afternoon: Thank you, Father, in these past twenty-four hours for:

- an awesome phone call with Holly
- the encouraging and affirming lunch with Jeff
- the appreciation for leading the Bible study expressed by my friend, Jon
- the prayer/walk at Marymoor Dog Park with good ol' Griffey
- the prayer on the phone with L. for his son in rehab
- the joy of hearing about Heidi, Sky, and their girls' family adventure to Hawaii
- the fellowship over dinner with Brad and Nita, visiting from Hawaii
- Your mom's successful surgery and good doctor visit
- Your mom telling me with joy about her Bible study leader, Cindy, whom she had lunch with, who provided a great dinner last night because of Mom's surgery

You get the picture. This was just in the past twenty-four hours, son. If I make the effort to recall these things, it does something to my attitude. I begin to see God as lovingly involved in my life. If there is one habit I have that I would also want you to adopt, this would be it. Son, it is so easy for me to act with negativity and feel entitled. That is so much the "old me." But I need to continually remind myself that Christ died for and with that "me" on the cross. He exchanged my life *with* His to give me a grateful "new me" life.

But you and I can only make this "new me" really come alive by daily walking in grateful obedience. Let me leave you with a verse of scripture that I have found very helpful: "So then, just as you received Christ Jesus as Lord, continue to live in him, rooted and built up in him, strengthened in the faith as you were taught, and *overflowing with thankfulness*" (Colossians 2:6–7, emphasis mine).

Growing in an attitude of gratitude,

Dad

Reflections on Thanksgiving

Dear Son,

I love our family Thanksgiving celebrations. Next to Christmas, Thanksgiving is my favorite holiday. I love how we go around the table and give thanks to God for something or someone for which we feel grateful. But as I suggested in my last letter on gratitude, Thanksgiving cannot be just a once-a-year thing, but rather should be a 365 day-per-year lifestyle. The apostle Paul hits on this a lot in his letters, because it seems like he wants our lives as Christ-followers to be saturated with gratitude.

Here's an example: "Be joyful always. Pray continually; give thanks *in all circumstances,* for this is God's will for you in Christ Jesus" (1 Thessalonians 5:16–18, emphasis mine).

Son, why does Paul emphasize gratitude so much? Here are three reasons that I can ascertain.

First, gratitude helps me affirm that my heavenly Father is always at work in my life (John 5:17), which makes me aware of His continual presence even when it may be hard to recognize Him otherwise. It elevates my concept of God. Thanksgiving takes God out of whatever box I have tried to put Him into in my mind, and helps me see a little more of His power, wisdom, and sovereign love that permeates my life everywhere.

Second, thanksgiving draws me closer to Him and helps me to avoid taking Him and His kindnesses for granted, while protecting me from falling into the trap of entitlement thinking.

Third, gratitude prevents me from being "problem centered," moving me to be more "Person centered," with that person being the triune God. It builds my confidence in what He will do in the future by reminding me and affirming what He has done in the past. I learn to thank Him before the answers to my prayers ever come. I try not to do this with presumption, but rather with a restful confidence that God will answer my prayers as He sees fit.

Son, you know me and you know my weaknesses. You know that I am not naturally a grateful person. I was born with this melancholy kind of personality that seems to naturally see the glass as half empty rather than half full. You remember me telling you how I lamented to your grandpa on my sixth birthday that "five of my best years were already over, never to ever return." Besides that internal tendency, I grew up in a world of abundance where I could always feel entitled to have just a little bit more! You also know the perpetuation of consumer-discontent is the fire that fuels a large part of our economy; it drives the engine so to speak.

However, you and I can't use our temperament or the economy as excuses. If we do, we will just pass on ingratitude to our children and grandchildren. Habit is formed by consistent choices, which become our character and then ultimately become our destiny. You and I must choose gratitude, not only for our own sakes, but for the legacy that we will pass on.

Forever grateful for you,

Dad

Believing Is Seeing

Dear Son,

We have all grown up with the motto, "seeing is believing." This materialistic and pragmatic worldview leads us to trust only what we have already verified with our own eyes. In this way of thinking, only fools believe *before* they see. But as followers of Christ, *we are called to do exactly that. It is called "walking by faith."*

Son, you will face many times in life when your faith will be tested. What you thought could or would never happen, will occur. You will be tempted to believe that you have been forgotten and neglected by God. Believe me, I wish only good things for you, but I know as God's man you will be tested to believe *before* you see, in different areas of life.

When this occurs, do not think for a moment you have been neglected by the Father. God did not forget Abraham when He led him up to Mount Moriah to test him with Isaac. Moses was not forsaken when he found himself facing the Red Sea, with Pharaoh's army bearing down upon the people he had led out of Egypt. David was not alone when he was chased around the countryside by a crazily jealous King Saul. These men, God's men, learned to believe before they saw God's deliverance or His answer to their prayers.

But this isn't just for Bible heroes, son. I have had to learn this, and I have walked with other Christian men who have had to learn these same excruciatingly hard lessons. Sometimes it involved a troubled marriage or a wayward child or a loss of job or a life-threatening disease. These are the kinds of things that God will use to graciously train us to develop eyes of faith that believe *before* we see.

In John 7:17 the Lord Jesus said it this way, "If anyone chooses to do God's will, he will find out whether my teaching comes from God or whether I speak on my own." In John 20:29, after His resurrection, He told Thomas, "Because you have seen me you have believed; blessed are those who have not seen and yet have believed."

Do you see the situation we are in, son? We live in a land where "seeing is believing," but we are called to follow a Lord who insists, "believing is seeing." This isn't easy!

I can remember a talk a man named Walt Henrichsen gave several years ago, while I was on staff with The Navigators. He said most of our faith walk is spent where we are like the audience in a theatre and the hand of God is at work behind a closed curtain. God is training us to walk by faith. He wants to grow our trust in Him, so that we learn to thank Him *before* we see the results of His work, without seeing what He is up to behind the curtain.

However, He is a gracious Father who knows our weaknesses, and there are certain times when He will pull back the curtain and give us a glimpse of what He is doing. Almost immediately He will then close the curtain and gently say to us, "Okay, you've had a glimpse of what I'm up to. Now continue to walk by faith."

So, son, this earthly journey, as joyful as it can be because we have the Lord with us always, is still like being in a dark theatre with the curtain closed. But here is what we can be assured of:

- He *is* at work behind the curtain.
- We are not alone in the theatre. He is with us, and He has placed others with us who are living the same believe-and-then-see lifestyle.
- Someday soon the curtain will be pulled back for good and our believing will be seeing forever.
- This time of waiting for believing to turn to seeing is a very short sliver of time in light of eternity.
- This believing-before-seeing way of life is developing in us Christ-like character and spiritual overcoming "muscles."
- He has great purpose for us, both in this life and the life to come.
- Most importantly, to believe, to trust, to thank God before we see what we hope for come about, brings glory and honor to *Him.*

Believing *is* seeing, son. Whatever challenge you are facing right now, be assured that it is temporary and the relationship with God that is being forged in the midst of it is eternal. He is being glorified as you learn to believe before you see. Remember, tough times never last but tough people do.

Seeing God at work in you,

Dad

Chapter 10

Hear My Heart about Sex

"When you start seeing what you are and what you are about, you will easily avoid the things you can do without."
—Charles Slagle

Some Thoughts about Sex

Dear Son,

You may have skipped ahead to get to this chapter wondering, "What is Dad going to say to me about sex?" I know what you are thinking, too. "I hope he doesn't talk about sex with Mom in this letter." Don't worry, I won't. What I want to leave you with is a metaphor. Sex is like fire. It is a wonderful gift that gives warmth and life, but if it is taken out of its proper place it can destroy like no other thing.

I have struggled with sexual temptation my entire adult life. I have had periods when I have not struggled as much or have had good self-control, but I have other times when I have succumbed to allowing myself to look at images that

I should not have. I regret every time I have fallen with that temptation, as that has detracted from being content with what God has provided for me to legitimately enjoy in my marriage.

Whether you are single or married, unfortunately you will find that sexual temptation will be with you the rest of your life. Of course you can give in to it and do what you want, but the cost of that is a life of wounded relationships, one or more broken marriages, wounded children, sexual addiction, guilt, shame, and distancing yourself from God. So I truly believe this is one area that you need to be honest about and deal with.

Proverbs says much about this. You may want to read a chapter a day from Proverbs for a season. You will be amazed at how much Solomon speaks to his sons about this issue. Of course he didn't exactly practice what he preached. The book of Ecclesiastes is a record of a broken man who indulged in sexual sin and paid the heavy price for it.

What I have found helpful is to be honest with another man whom you can trust about where you are sexually. Ask him to pray for you in this area, so that you don't develop a dark, secret part of your life that you keep partitioned off from the rest of the world. I have found James 5:16 to be very helpful for me.

What is accessible today on the Internet is mind boggling. The big business of pornography financially drives the Internet. What the explosion of technology has meant for men (and women) is that we can privately and "secretly" access images seemingly without any risk of being discovered or caught. This has been so destructive to men and their marriages, not to mention its effect on women, and the treatment of women as sexual objects.

Once this bait is taken and it becomes "food" through a steady diet of pornography and masturbation, a whole series of unintended consequences follow, and these *unintended* consequences are what kill. Here are just a few:

- Unhealthy and unfair comparison of your wife to someone or something she could never compete with results in diminished satisfaction and increased criticism
- Selfish obsession with sexual release—it becomes about me—carries over into the marital sexual relationship
- Perverse images that cannot be easily erased from the brain's "hard drive"
- Guilt and shame and a sense of condemnation
- Loss of spiritual hunger as emptiness is sought to be filled through sexual escape and fantasy
- Diminishing returns that act like a drug taking ever-greater perversion to stimulate and gratify
- Addiction, a sense of not being able to stop

I'm sure there are more consequences, but you get the picture.

This is far too strong a force to be fought toe-to-toe. The patriarch, Joseph, gave us a good picture of how to deal with this temptation: R-u-n! I have found that I need to have a friend that I can be honest with in this area who will pray for me.

In my marriage I need to do all I can to keep the romance alive, so that we can enjoy each other sexually. When we do, we aren't just "roommates." Sorry, I forgot: Don't picture that one. Just take the principle and leave the imagery alone.☺

I want you to have a great sex life in your marriage. This is one of the great gifts the Lord has for us on this earth. That is why I am giving you these warnings, son. Sex is a gift to be fully enjoyed with your wife someday, but know that we do have an enemy who desires to "steal and kill and destroy" (John 10:10), and he will twist this gift that is part of the abundant life to our destruction if we let him. Thanks for listening, son.

Because this is *really* important,

Dad

Some More Thoughts about Sex

Dear Son,

I can still hear that Rascals' song ringing in my ears from the summer of '68:

All the world over, so easy to see,
people everywhere just wanna be free.

For many in my generation this freedom meant freedom from moral restraint, and freedom to enjoy "recreational sex," drugs, or whatever felt good in the moment. Though this philosophy was seductively appealing on the surface, it led to slavery and death, not just for my generation, but for every society throughout history who has ever tried it.

Son, today the battle to be free, to be *truly free*, from the tyranny of sin is more challenging than ever. Pornography can be so easily accessed on the cell phone, computer, and television. This is not the only addiction that men (and women) struggle with; there are those who struggle with drugs, alcohol, food, work, gambling, and excessive watching of sports.

You may be wondering how to recognize if you have become enslaved. Here are a few questions you can ask yourself:

- Do I feel powerfully and consistently drawn to it, and feel helpless to stop even if I wanted to?

- Is this something that is separating me from having a closer relationship to God or my family?
- Is this something my father modeled to me? As sons, we are particularly tempted in the areas that our fathers may have been tempted to use to numb their pain.

I have often thought in protest, *So what if I can identify an area of addiction? What harm does a little crutch, escape, or diversion do?*

The answer that I have found, son, is that it will hurt the most important people in my life—my wife and my children. If I use these things for my own gratification in this painful world, there is less of "me" to offer to them. This also goes for my relationship with God. By nibbling on the junk food of my addiction of choice, I "spoil my appetite" for the perfectly satisfying meal of fellowship with God.

So, son, the challenge is to experience freedom from being in bondage to things that God gave us to enjoy in the right context. If that something has a hold on me in a way that I can't stop even though I want to, if it is hindering my relationship with God and my family and has become a source of control over me, then I need to deal with it.

When I have been in this situation, and come to my senses about it, I cry out to God and admit that I have become enslaved by it. I ask forgiveness for allowing this thing to come between me and Him. As you know, my favorite verse in the Bible is Galatians 2:20: "I have been crucified with Christ and I no longer live, but Christ lives in me. The life I live in the body, I live by faith in the Son of God, who loved me and gave himself for me." I pray these words to the Father and reaffirm who I am as His son, indwelt by His Son, Jesus Christ, and that I'm fully dependent upon His life in me through His Spirit.

I have learned over and over again how weak my willpower is. So don't allow yourself to be shamed into giving up the fight, no matter how many times you fall. His grace and forgiveness are sufficient. He knows our weakness and our frailty. His blood is sufficient. His grace is sufficient. His love is more than sufficient.

Yet here's a warning, son: Don't fall into the trap of sinning willfully and presuming on God's grace. That is the devil's trap. I have gone down that path. The problem is, though God's mercy is limitless, the law of sowing and reaping is always in operation. Galatians 6:7-8 tells us, "Do not be deceived: God cannot be mocked. A man reaps what he sows. The one who sows to please his sinful nature, from that nature will reap destruction; the one who sows to please the Spirit, from the Spirit will reap eternal life."

God sees our hearts. If we have hearts to do what pleases Him, to keep pursuing Him, to remove obstacles and temptations when we become aware of them, He will be amazingly patient with us. As He promises in 1 Corinthians 10:13, *He will provide a way to stand against the temptation.* Second Timothy 2:22 tells us that He will give us a band of brothers to help us continue our pursuit of closeness to Him. And James 5:16 assures us that He will lead us to at least one confidant to whom we can confess, and who will pray with us for healing. He promises that He will keep picking us up and dusting us off.

I hope you hear my heart: This is a *battle.* The fight will come to you, whether you want it to or not. It will not get easier as you get older. Determine to fight, son, but use God's weapons: the cross of Christ where the "old you" died with Him, the presence of God through His Spirit, your Christian brothers who want to live pure lives as well, and the cleansing blood of Christ to wash you every time you fall. Be smart and put some protections in place for yourself so you are not setting yourself up to fall. I heard a man in recovery from alcohol addiction say, "If you sit in a barber's chair long enough, you will wind up with a haircut."

> All the world over, so easy to see,
> people everywhere just wanna be free.

You and I can live more free than those who seek freedom through indulging their every desire. It is a freedom that Christ gives, and it is experienced only as we give *ourselves fully to Him first, then* to others as a servant. Galatians 5:13 states, "You, my brothers, were called to be free. But do not use your freedom to indulge the sinful nature; rather, serve one another in love."

Growing in freedom,

Dad

Chapter 11

You Aren't What
You Do or Have

"Sometimes the poorest man leaves his children the richest inheritance."
—Ruth E. Renkel

Balancing Work and Family Life

Dear Son,

One of the biggest battles you are going to fight is how to balance work and family. This is a growing problem in America where husbands and wives, dads and moms are not able to give "their best selves" to their families. Work life bleeds into family life and robs it of rest and joy. The phenomenon has been described as "the rising pressure to invest more of one's energy in work at the expense of family."

You grew up in "Microsoft-land" and you know that my work with fathers was much about helping them remember that the greatest "presents" dads can give their children is their "presence."

Of course, before the Industrial Revolution, work and family were integrated and the home, which was a center for family production, not a center of consumption. Work then actually drew the family together rather than kept them apart.

Son, as challenging as these external realities are, I believe the greatest conflict you will face is internal. We have a very real enemy of our souls and he will deceive us to falling into the "comparison trap" whenever he can. He has a very compliant ally in this battle—our own sinful selves! Comparison drives us in our work lives and tempts us to feel perpetually dissatisfied, because we are constantly comparing ourselves to "ghosts." These "ghosts" could be those of our fathers or grandfathers and what they did for a living, the images in our media, from our peers, siblings, co-workers, or neighbors.

If you think about it, most often the first thing people ask when meeting someone new is, "What do you do?" There is a legitimate motivation for asking such a question as it provides a way to relate and connect, but the question has a more sinister side to it as well. It is bathed in the acid of comparison.

"What do you do?" can be heard as "How important are you?" I have always envied the guys who can just simply say, "I'm a surgeon" or "I'm the CEO of a Fortune-500 Company" or "As a matter of fact I AM a rocket scientist!" Those jobs carry lots of prestige and don't need much explanation.

The problem with seeing what we do for work through comparison glasses is that it makes us feel insecure, like being precariously perched on a razor-thin ridge, in danger of falling off either side.

On one side is the lie of my own superiority. That happens when I see myself as better than others based on what I do for a living. That can fuel and drive me to try to continue to maintain this false sense of superiority. I become a slave to this "god" that gives me what I want. My best energies will go to where this god is served, which is the workplace. As I over-commit, my wife, and eventually my children, will receive only my "emotional leftovers."

On the other side of this ridge is the lie of my inferiority. If I view the work that I do in comparison to others as less valuable to God or to my family, then I slide down the slippery slope into the devil's trap of believing in my inferiority, which leads to self-condemnation and eventually despair. No matter how hard I work, no matter how I use my God-given talents, I see the work I do as having little value.

I have struggled with this one. Since my thirties, I have chosen to pursue work in the non-profit arena, first with The Navigators and later through our family foundation. This isn't particularly prestigious or lucrative. But I have learned to ignore my "inner voices of comparison" and remind myself of my call that I clearly heard from God as a twenty-year-old. As I partner with your mom in this ministry, I sense I am doing exactly what I am destined to do, no matter what criticisms or misunderstandings I may encounter. This hasn't been easy, but this has been my journey.

That has been my experience and it is much different from that of my grandfathers, my father, and what you will choose to do. You must find your own way, son. I am confident that you will.

Son, just remember *you aren't what you do!* A job or career cannot become your identity because it can be changed or lost at any time. If you find yourself in a season where you are under-employed, unemployed, searching for work, or dissatisfied with your current job, realize that this can be a time God is using to remind you where your true identity is as a son of the heavenly Father.

> Proud of who you *are* no matter what you happen to *do,*
>
> Dad

Facing Financial Pressure

Dear Son,

I know that you have felt financial stress and pressure. And you see people stressed out about their finances all around you. You have seen bankruptcies and foreclosures as an everyday occurrence in what is now known as *The Great Recession.* Our federal government has lived way outside of its means, and we have a major debt problem that has huge implications for our nation's future.

Financial pressure is something that you have faced and will continue to face as you move through adulthood.

Son, as you know, what is becoming common in America is for people to use credit cards as a safety net for tough financial times. When the cards get maxed out, they then begin to tap into the equity in their homes. As the costs of health care, education, fuel, and mortgage payments increase, families find themselves in a cycle of unnecessary punitive fees and interest rates. It is a trap. Stay out of it if at all possible!

But if you ever find yourself going backwards financially, the sooner you honestly face the situation the better. To delay facing the consequences just deepens the hole of debt that you will need to be dug out of. To stay "in the dark" will only add to the stress.

If you have credit card debt, the first thing is to create a plan to pay off the cards, prioritizing them with the card bearing the highest interest payment first.

Then, if you need it, seek help. I highly recommend the "Financial Peace University™." Many young couples, like your sister, Heidi and her husband, Sky, have gone through it, and it has helped them tremendously to get on the same page and on solid financial footing. The program helps with practical things like putting together a budget.

To this point you have been really good at *not* over-spending. You have learned that one way to cut your expenditures is to not eat out too frequently. Having worked in the restaurant business, you know that the average markup of a restaurant meal is about three times the cost of the food.

If you haven't started a savings account, it is never too late to start that discipline. As Heidi and Sky have done, you can create special savings accounts for different things, like gifts, repairs, or vacations.

I am confident that you know this stuff. And I see that you are doing well. If you fall down in an area, just get back up and learn from it. We all struggle with financial choices. We all make mistakes. I have sure made my share of them. But this is an area worth focusing on. When your finances are under control, there is great peace and satisfaction and a sense of security within your heart and your home.

Seeing you financially free,

Dad

Consumed by Consumption

Dear Son,

Materialism is one of the legacies that my generation has passed on to yours. We Baby Boomers, and those who have come after us, did not hear "No" very much when it came to our spending.

Many of us have passed on a sense of entitlement to our children. As I wrote in my last letter, debt is a huge problem for families today. Consumer credit and mortgage debt are both at a higher percentage of disposable income in America than ever before. In other words, what families owe versus what they are worth has never been so high. We have lost sight of the concept of savings and delayed gratification and have opted out for debt and instant gratification.

Remember when we played "spot the lie" as we watched Super Bowl commercials together, when I gave you a quarter for every lie you could identify? I was fighting materialism with materialism! For example, the lie in a beer ad may be, "If you drink our beer you will have beautiful women attracted to you." That is what we need to continue to do when it comes to this craziness. We need to consciously identify the lies that the media constantly bombards us with.

Also, son, we cannot just "play defense" in this. The best way to keep a healthy focus in this area is through serving others and practicing generosity. You remember our family mission trips to Mexico and Central America? As a family, we could learn to bless those who have less materially. That latest video game or gadget doesn't seem so vitally important to have when you have just helped put a roof over the heads of a family of six for the first time in their lives.

You are not what you do *and* you are not what you have. The more stuff we have, the more we have to take care of, and the more that the stuff we own has the potential to ultimately own us. I know that you know this. This is just a reminder. We have not always done real well with this, but at least we have engaged in the battle.

In His grace,

Dad

Chapter 12

Last But Not Least

"*The golden rule of understanding spiritually is not intellect but obedience. If a man wants scientific knowledge, intellectual curiosity is his guide; but if he wants insight into what Jesus teaches, he can only get it by obedience.*"
—Oswald Chambers

The Parable of the River

Dear Son,

You know I love to kayak in the summer down the rivers of the Cascade Mountains. There is something about the sparkling beauty of these rivers on a lazy Pacific Northwest summer afternoon that takes my breath away.

One time recently I paddled down the Snoqualmie River with my friend, Tom. As we drove out together, I felt the need to "process" with him about some frustrations I was having at the time. What I love about Tom is that he is a guy who really listens. He doesn't try to fix me or give me simplistic answers to perplexing problems. There are some guys who make you feel stupid because you haven't figured out how to fix your own problems, when they offer their simple solutions in a mere fraction of the time you have thought and prayed over them!

One thing Tom did tell me about was something he had been reading that was helpful to him. It was an article by the late Henri Nouwen. When I got home I read it. Ironically, the very activity that Tom and I were doing, paddling down a river, became a visual illustration of Nouwen's message. He was talking about three things that are essential for our spiritual health and growth—solitude, community, and ministry.

He used Jesus as the supreme model of what each of us needs to do for this kind of spiritual health. Jesus repeatedly went to the mountainside to be alone with His Father. Solitude was essential to Him. Just as a river's very life begins in the "solitude," in the quiet of the snow-packed mountaintops, so does our spiritual life.

Son, this element of solitude is so important in our noisy, high tech, information-saturated world of today. Since Jesus, the God-Man, found it necessary to carve out regular times of solitude, early in the morning, away from the crowds or in the mountains, how much more do we. He did this regularly, I believe, because He needed to be reminded He was "beloved" by the Father.

I know that when I have not had enough quiet, alone time with God, just with me and my Bible opened up to His presence and His voice speaking to me personally, I begin to get "spiritual amnesia," a certain forgetfulness of who He is and who I am as His beloved son.

As I reflect upon that paddle trip with Tom, I realize all of the benefits that we reveled in on the river began in the "solitude" of a snowcapped mountain. The melted snow flowed eventually into the river we enjoyed. This is the place from which all blessings flowed.

Nouwen's article continued with the next step: community. It is interesting that Jesus, after His retreat from people, always moved right back into community. In His case His community was His disciples. Community can be messy. It can be turbulent at times. Community life is pictured by the upper parts of the river, where water cascades over and around boulders creating dangerous rapids. This portion of the river is paradoxically treacherous, yet also gushes with life.

I believe that community is first lived out in the context of the family. It is full of dangers, conflicts, and great joy all at the same time. In family, we inevitably experience disagreements, misunderstandings, and wounded feelings. But we are also forced to practice forbearance, kindness, and patience, if true community is to survive and ultimately thrive.

Son, Lord willing, you will lead a family community someday, beginning with you and your wife, and then your children. Growing up in our home, you have seen both the sinful chaos and the redemptive joy of our family community. Though our family was far from perfect, I hope you know that any good you experienced didn't just happen by accident. We are still together, still committed to each other, because we practiced forbearance, forgiveness, and patience. Without these we would be torn apart, crushed on the boulders. But we have hung on through the rapids. Our life as a family has given you a legacy you can build upon, and hopefully improve upon when you start your own family.

As the river moves down the mountain, it shifts from these rapids to a broader, gentler flow into the valley below. This represents what Nouwen wrote about Jesus: He always helped His community move toward ministry, to serving the needs of others.

Jesus and His disciples walked together and touched those in the crowd who came to Him. Ministry just "flowed" naturally from Him and His disciples. A river humbly flows downward to give life to the thirsty land below. It provides its life-giving presence, and that is enough.

Son, I have come to realize that I have to keep my eyes focused on others and away from just meeting my own needs if I am to keep growing in my faith. Vibrant spiritual life originates in solitude, flows into the chaos of community, and then flows out into ministry. So don't just live for yourself. Serve others. Just like a river gives life to everything it touches, we can, too, if we make ourselves available to others and meet their needs when we can. There is great joy in that. This has been just a gentle, fatherly reminder, as I know you already know this.

Please think about this river analogy that God has given us in nature. It has helped me and I know it will help you.

> With gratitude to Him through whom all blessings flow,
>
> Dad

Backpacks and Boulders

Dear Son,

Now that you are a young adult, I am learning to let go of you. This isn't an easy process. You will discover that someday, when you are a father in my season of life. There is a concept that I have been learning in a small group that I will call "Backpacks and Boulders."

As adults, each of us has our "backpack" to carry, our normal, daily responsibilities to our spouse, if we are married, to our children, if we are a parent, to our employer, and to others with whom we are in relationship. And as a man of faith, you know that I believe that we are each responsible to God, to be in right relationship with Him, to respond to His grace. These are all simply normal human burdens or weights we are called on to carry as "backpacks."

There are also times when we are in situations in our lives that we are called to carry "boulders." These cannot be carried alone. We need others to help us bear a weight that would be too crushing to shoulder alone.

As your dad, I have sought to teach you how to carry your "backpack." I am proud of you for the way that you have stepped up and become responsible for the things that only you can carry. I will let you in on a struggle that I have had as you move into young adulthood. I often forget that your "backpack" is not a "boulder." I want to come in and help you carry whatever it is at the moment. By doing that, I can actually hinder you from carrying your own load and growing into the man God has called you to be.

Please forgive me for nagging too much about your spiritual journey. I know you are on your own journey, and it won't be the same as mine. You have your own unique relationship with God, and you are sorting out what is real and what is not real for you. This is a sacred process. I respect that and honor the journey God has for *you*.

Also, as I look at things like finding your vocation and choosing a lifetime mate, which are backpacks only you can carry, there is something in me that wants to meddle here, too, as you have seen my tendencies. But I promise I won't. Instead, I will encourage you, because for me to try to help you carry them would hurt and not help, and that is the last thing I ever want to do.

You will have your "boulders." When they come, I believe that you and I will know the difference. I will be there to help you shoulder the extra load when it comes. I think that being an active grandparent is part of this, and your mom and I won't mind it at all.

One thing I commit to you, son, until the day I die, and probably afterwards, because I think prayer is still a big part of heaven as I understand it, is that I will always hold you up in my prayers. And that is no burden to me at all. It is part of the backpack I gladly carry.

With joy,

Dad

Detecting the Lie

Dear Son,

Ready or not, here comes another river analogy. Last fall I spent a really special time on the Green River with Pastor Brad, while he was on vacation from Hawaii. The air was crystal clear, fragrant with all of the autumn smells, and the temperature was perfect. The river water was sparkling clear, with a slightly green hue as we paddled along on that lazy September afternoon.

As we glided down the river, pink salmon were swimming up from the ocean, thousands of them, right under our kayaks! Salmon coming back to spawn is truly a miracle. Remember when we saw them come through the fish ladder at the Ballard locks when you were little? We learned that these seemingly dumb fish go out into the sea from a stream and several years later swim all the way back to where they came from, through every conceivable barrier, to spawn and die. How they do this is way beyond me! Truly, this is just another one of God's amazing wonders in His creation.

Pastor Brad, always the avid fisherman, was really fascinated by a river full of fish. I asked him if it was a good idea to try to catch them, and he informed me that they were already "humping," or forming an ugly hump on their backs, indicating that they were not good to eat, kind of mushy I guess. He told me that they could legally be caught downstream before they got into that condition as long as the fisherman had a license and kept to his limit.

I then asked Brad, "How do you catch these fish? Do you just reach in with your hand and pull them out?" That is apparently legal, but not very sporting! The normal way to catch fish, using bait that is an attractive food, does not work for these salmon when they are making their way up river. The reason is that they are coming up the river single-mindedly to spawn and die, and they are not interested in eating. I guess food doesn't have the same appeal when you are getting near death. Maybe it would be like offering peanuts and crackers to the passengers when the *Titanic* was sinking.

As I have struggled with sin as an adult, I think this image of fish going after bait is a good one. Generally, we sin because we are fooled to believe that what is offered as bait will fulfill a hunger that we have, like hungry fish lunging at the deceptive promise of a fisherman's bait.

As I seek to be less and less fooled and pulled by the bait that the enemy throws out to me, I need to learn to "detect the lie" that is packed around the deadly hook that looks and smells like a harmless morsel of food. I have found that if I learn to detect the lie that is overlaying the destructive habit or harmful behavior, it is increasingly easier for me to keep from falling for it. If you and I can grow in this kind of wisdom we will be like a "bait-wise" fish who has learned to pass on those little "happy meals" that are really just too good (and costly) to be true.

Happily hooked on Jesus,

Dad

Cleaning Off the Barnacles

Dear Son,

Early in your Grandpa Bo's retirement from Sambo's, after we moved to Hawaii, he owned a fifty-foot sailboat. Maybe it could be said more accurately that it owned him. He kept this beautiful teak-covered ketch at the yacht club in Kaneohe Bay. It was called *The Moonraker,* and it gave our family some wonderful memories. My favorite times were when he took the boat to the outer islands. To be honest though, getting there wasn't that much fun; I usually got seasick on the way.

To sail along the lush white sandy beach shores, and camp out on a boat that gently rocked me to sleep, was as close to living in paradise as I think I've ever experienced.

At first your grandpa enjoyed maintaining his boat, but eventually I know he tired of the constant upkeep it required in the tropical, salty air of Kaneohe Bay. He used to quote, "The two happiest days of a boat owner's life are the day he buys it and the day he sells it!" He didn't have to concern himself only with the damage that the sun and salt did above the waterline, but he had to worry about the little shelled creatures that attached themselves to submerged areas of the boat's hull.

These creatures, known as barnacles, are a shell species that release millions of larvae. The sea creatures attach themselves to solid, non-moving objects, such as docked boats, where they can absorb nutrients that float through the water. The chemicals secreted by the organisms also cause damage and add drag to the hull, reducing its speed and efficiency.

So your poor ol' grandpa would constantly have to concern himself with these little boat-fouling freeloaders, either through putting on a snorkel and mask to scrub the hull while docked, or by taking his boat out of the water and putting it into dry dock for scraping, sanding, and repainting.

Son, as you know, I have been following Christ since I was seventeen years old. The one message that I have heard over and over is that if I allow anything to be added to a simple trust in Christ and His sufficiency alone, then I am allowing spiritual barnacles to form. In effect, by adding anything onto Christ, I am subtracting, slowing down my progress, being weighed down and being hindered in my journey.

These spiritual barnacles are subtle and hard to detect. Sometimes they come in the form of how much of a sense of "righteousness" I receive from what I do, rather than simply relying on who God says I am. Sometimes they come in the form of how much I rely on my circumstances, my subjective feelings, and others' feedback, rather than simply trusting in Christ's righteousness on my behalf alone.

Son, I have found that this reliance on "doing" and the seeking of approval and validation from others are *my* barnacles. They are hidden below the waterline in areas where I trust in "Christ plus"—Christ plus a good reputation, Christ plus positive response from others, Christ plus performance, Christ plus!

I have found that like actual barnacles, I need to bring these spiritual barnacles into the sunlight of God's truth about me and allow Jesus' special cleansing blood solution to be generously applied.

Seeking to sail barnacle-free,

Dad

Home Alone

Dear Son,

This is the last letter of this little book I have compiled. I want to close with an honest disclosure: I wrestle with loneliness. That is why it has been especially hard for me to see you and your siblings leave home. Although I know this is what you were raised up to do, the emptying of the nest has been hard for me to deal with. I have wrestled off and on with feelings of depression as the realization that the end of the active, child-raising years has slowly sunk in.

I trust you remember how the family movie "Home Alone" became an instant hit during the holiday season in the early nineties. If you recall, the film was about a precocious eight-year-old boy named Kevin McCallister, played by Macaulay Culkin. Kevin is accidentally left home alone when his family, late for their flight, madly rushes off to Paris for the Christmas holidays without him. The fun of the movie is watching little Kevin cleverly use booby traps against two bumbling burglars who are trying to break into his home.

If you look more closely at Kevin and his family dynamics, he was actually "home alone" long before the family accidentally left him behind. Even when he was in the house with his parents and siblings, he was clearly alienated from them. Being alone is not primarily a physical situation but a condition of the soul.

Being "home alone" started with our ancestors Adam and Eve, and we have been feeling it ever since. As a man, I first looked to your mom to fill my void of loneliness, and then I looked to you and your siblings. But even the best of times in family relationships, as blessed as they may be, cannot fill the void. They were never meant to.

If I try to run away from it or deny it, I wind up demanding from others what only God can provide. The more I demand, the angrier and lonelier I will feel.

Unlike Kevin in the movie, my greatest enemy is not a couple of incompetent burglars wanting to invade my home, but one fully competent thief who is already there—me, myself, and I. To be specific, it is the "old me" who still demands his selfish needs be met; he is my greatest threat.

I am slowly learning, son, to turn away from this seemingly very much alive "me" who the Bible says actually died with Christ. I am also learning to look to my Savior to meet my deepest longings. He is freeing me to increasingly see your mom, your siblings, and you as gifts He has given to me to love and to treasure. I am learning to see that the family life we enjoyed under one roof was just a part of the *journey*. It is not the *final destination*.

I know that when I remember this, I will help bring a greater sense of God's presence into our family. Yes, in one sense I am experiencing those "Home Alone" feelings, but in a greater sense I am not, because I am not really "home" yet!

> Looking forward to sharing this
> ongoing life journey with you,
>
> Dad

WinePressPublishing
Great Books, Defined.

To order additional copies of this book call:
1-877-421-READ (7323)
or please visit our website at
www.WinePressbooks.com

If you enjoyed this quality custom-published book,
drop by our website for more books and information.

www.winepresspublishing.com
"Your partner in custom publishing."

CPSIA information can be obtained at www.ICGtesting.com
Printed in the USA
BVOW081525070912

299742BV00001B/55/P